HR and Marketing
Power Partners

HR and Marketing Power Partners

the competitive advantage that will transform your business and establish a culture of performance

Pat Nazemetz
Will Ruch

CONTENTS

Foreword

Anne M. Mulcahy
Former Chairman and CEO, Xerox Corporation

Not many CEOs have résumés that include being the head of Human Resources. I am pleased to be a member of that elite group. What I learned from my tenure in HR proved invaluable to me when I became CEO. It also shaped my expectations of HR and its leader.

I had started my Xerox career in sales and followed a typical career path. I knew a lot about our customers, our products and how to lead a successful sales organization. But it wasn't until I moved into HR, first as Director of HR Operations and then as Chief Human Resource Officer (CHRO), that I understood the enterprise as a whole. I credit my tenure in HR for helping me to see the big picture. It also reinforced what I had learned in sales: At the end of the day, a company is only as good as its people.

When I headed HR, people would ask what my HR strategy was. My response, then and now, is that HR doesn't need a strategy. There is only the business strategy. Some people were disappointed by my position, arguing that HR had to have its own strategic vision to prove its worth to the enterprise.

An HR strategy isn't the best way to go about it. I believe you can be strategic about HR without having an HR strategy. The latter runs the risk of detracting from the business strategy. It's too easy to get caught up in the minutiae of traditional HR processes. They aren't ends in themselves, but rather the means to achieve the goals of the business. The best HR professionals always look at HR processes through the lens of the business strategy.

HR is most effective when its work dovetails with the business strategy. HR must focus on what's important to the business, what will drive the business forward. And that's talent. It fuels the business strategy and brings it to life.

That's what I believed as CHRO, and I was absolutely sure of it as CEO. In that role, I was privileged to have Pat Nazemetz as my CHRO. And we made a great team. A true HR professional, Pat has an amazing intellect. Her innovative thinking on health care garnered her national recognition. She went on to apply that same creativity to other aspects of total pay. But Pat's real passion, where she found the greatest satisfaction, is talent.

I depended on Pat to manage Xerox's people agenda. She was my counselor and confidante on everything related to our people. She knows what it takes to build a talent-driven organization, from new college hires to executives. Pat understood how to create the right work environment, how to engage people and how to align them to the goals of the business.

Here's the most important message I have for today's CHROs. *You own the talent plank of the business strategy.* It's your highest responsibility and your greatest leverage. And it's where you can add the greatest value to the enterprise.

Adding value is the key. At the Society for Human Resource Management (SHRM) conference in San Antonio in 2010, I talked with a number of CHROs. Inevitably, the conversations came around to the subject of a "seat at the table." Some disciplines have an automatic seat at the table: the President or Chief Operating Officer, the Chief Financial Officer, the General Counsel, the Controller. They get a bye. HR, on the other hand, always seems to be on the bubble. For CHROs, the chances of getting a seat at the table are directly related to the value they add to the enterprise. Pat earned her seat at the table by delivering on the talent agenda, which ultimately included working with and preparing my successor, Ursula Burns.

Like me, Pat has recently retired from Xerox. But she hasn't retired from HR. Instead, she's looking to share what she learned from 30 plus years in the field. Pat has partnered with Will Ruch, CEO of Versant, a communications and marketing firm, to produce this volume. Will worked with Pat during her last several years at Xerox, focusing on effective communication. His expertise in branding and marketing brought a whole new dimension, not just to communications, but to the way we looked at the role of HR.

Pat's deep knowledge of HR and Will's experience in marketing communications make for a powerful combination. They have collaborated to explore a compelling new concept: an alliance between HR and Marketing. One focuses on the workplace, the other on the marketplace. Looking at them together in partnership offers real payoffs for both. The same brand that sells the product can be an effective talent magnet. And employees who understand the power of the brand can become ambassadors. Think of it as branding from the inside out.

Pat and Will have tapped into some thought leaders, current and former CHROs and CMOs, who generously shared their innovative ideas and practices. You can learn from their experience and add value to your business.

Business today is anything but business as usual; the economic arena is in a constant state of flux. The recession, globalization, currency trends, demographic shifts create problems. HR has to wrestle with these and other issues; good HR heads are always open to innovative ways to harness talent for the benefit of the business.

As CHRO, you are the steward entrusted to safeguard your company's greatest asset. Your CEO is counting on you to engage people, unleash their potential and empower them to deliver the goals of the enterprise. I think you've got the best job in the company, and I wish you every success.

Anne M. Mulcahy
June 2012

Preface

Will Ruch
President & CEO, Versant Solutions

This book about the power of partnerships is the product of a partnership. For the better part of a decade, I worked with Pat Nazemetz in her role as VP of Human Resources at Xerox Corporation. During that time we found that our skills and our perspectives were not just compatible but almost perfectly complementary.

With a 30-year career in HR, Pat had developed a deep understanding of people and their expectations of an employer. She was focused on engaging employees to elicit what she called their discretionary effort, the same kind of effort coaches talk about when they urge their players to give 110%.

I come from a marketing background, and I'm all about the brand. The image a company projects to customers is its most visible asset—and its most valuable. Companies make substantial investments in building, extending and revitalizing their brands. Chief Marketing Officers (CMOs) and their teams obsess on the best ways to engage customers.

So why not apply some of those marketing techniques to engage employees around the brand? Why not enlist them as brand ambassadors?

We discovered that Pat's HR background and my Marketing orientation dovetailed perfectly when it came to working on ways to engage employees. In our years of working together, we came to understand intuitively the power of building an organization with the right people and communicating the right messages to them.

Communications to employees don't have to be expensive or elaborate to be effective. But just as with Marketing, the messages do have to be carefully thought out. And they must be sincere. To achieve its end, communication has to be clear and articulate. More important—and this is where Marketing can really make a difference—it should resonate on an emotional level. Convincing employees' minds is one thing; persuading their hearts is quite another.

After Pat retired, we looked for ways to continue our collaboration. Writing about HR and Marketing and how their partnership can benefit both disciplines seemed to be a natural. Shortly after our initial discussions, I came across an article in *Harvard Business Review* (October 11, 2010) that confirmed we were on to something big. The author was Bill Taylor, co-founder of *Fast Company* and writer of *HBR*'s popular management blog. He recalled the message he delivered to a conference of marketing executives organized by the American Bankers Association. "You can't really think about your bank's customers, I argued, unless you also think about your bank's *people*."

In that same article, Taylor went on to say:

> The new "power couple" inside the best companies, I concluded, was an iron-clad partnership between marketing leadership and HR leadership. Your brand is your culture, your culture is your brand.

I couldn't have said it better myself. HR focuses on the right people—hiring, engaging and developing the talent needed for the business. Marketing is relentless about getting out the right message. Put the two together and you've got a formidable force that works to the advantage of both—not to mention the company as a whole.

We had a great idea, but we needed proof sources. Both Pat and I recognized the power of examples to help people see things differently, to understand how making some changes could benefit them. So we reached out—Pat to her CHRO counterparts, and I to my network of colleagues and clients. We found others who understood the power of marketing to employees, engaging them as brand ambassadors. We identified advocates of employer branding. We connected with both CHROs and CMOs, along with CEOs, from a wide range of industries. We invited entrepreneurs and people dedicated to leadership development to participate. From diverse backgrounds, industries and functions, these individuals and their partners share an intuitive understanding of the benefits of bringing together the discipline of HR and the creativity of Marketing.

More than two dozen contributors made this book possible. They generously shared their insights and experiences. We invite you to learn from them.

Acknowledgments

We started this project with an idea, that there is a sweet spot where Human Resources and Marketing intersect, where both disciplines can work together for their mutual benefit and make a difference in both the workplace and the marketplace. Having worked together as partners for a number of years, we saw this project as an opportunity to share our idea with a wider audience of HR and Marketing professionals.

Going from our original idea to the reality of the book in your hands (or on your screen) involved a great many more people. First, and most important, is our group of contributors. We were fortunate enough to identify more than two dozen thought leaders who served as proof sources for our thesis. They openly shared their views and experiences, expanding on and adding credibility to the original concept. We had the idea for this book, but our contributors had the big *ideas* that made the book possible. Our heartfelt thanks to the leaders who participated in our project and their organizations; we couldn't have done it without you.

Although not a contributor in the usual sense, Anne Mulcahy made an extraordinary contribution to our project. As both a former CHRO and CEO, she brings a unique perspective to the importance of the people agenda. She graciously volunteered to write the Foreword to share her thoughts with our readership. We thank her for enthusiastic participation.

Our very special thanks go to Paula Fleming, our writer extraordinaire. Without Paula, there would be no book. She developed the questions and conducted the interviews with each of our contributors. Then she worked her magic to craft chapters that read like personal conversations.

Over the years, we have had the opportunity to know and work with Paula. She has an amazing ability to combine her great intellect with brilliant writing skills and a passion to keep things simple and memorable. Thank you, Paula, for this wonderful end-product! We asked Paula to reflect on the process of working with us and our contributors; she shares her thoughts in the Afterword on page 225.

Finally, we thank the members of the Versant team that shepherded the book through the critical path to publication, distribution and marketing. Their creativity and skill added enormously to the quality of the book.

Pat Nazemetz & Will Ruch

Introduction

Patricia M. Nazemetz
Former CHRO, Xerox Corporation

I spent my entire career in HR because I knew that's where I could make the greatest impact. A company can have terrific products, a sound business plan and an eye-catching marketing campaign—and still not achieve greatness. Strategy and tactics don't matter much if the people in the organization can't execute the plan and deliver the results. What sets great companies apart from good or mediocre enterprises is their people. And for companies in the services business—everything from entry-level employees in call centers to Ph.D. actuarial consultants—their people *are* their product.

Here's the way I see it. The CEO and the Strategy group determine the plan beforehand, and Finance keeps score after the fact. Everything in between depends on the people in the organization. That's where HR can exert influence, both directly and indirectly. By attracting and retaining talent, by developing people to their fullest potential and especially by creating the right environment.

A lot of people outside HR think the function is just about pay and benefits. They're part of the equation, of course. Mary Eckenrod at RIM calls them table stakes; Tom Maddison, my successor at Xerox, uses the term boundary conditions. In a nutshell: necessary but far from sufficient. If you want to inspire people to perform at their best, you have to look at the whole environment.

HR is clearly responsible for programs and practices around comp, benefits, development, performance evaluation, reward and recognition. That's the technical content of our discipline, and we have to do it well. If these are designed and implemented in an environment where people are valued and work has meaning, it's possible to inspire loyalty, commitment and discretionary effort.

For the majority of jobs today, people who are beyond the learning curve can meet the requirements of their positions with something less than 100 percent of their effort. On the other hand, while mathematically improbable, I think that each of us is capable of reaching down and coming up with something more than 100 percent of the effort that could be expended. Someone once described this discretionary effort as the energy and enthusiasm of the first day on the job, combined with the productivity of the last day before vacation. Although it may not be a steady or constant state, if we can inspire people to tap into even a small part of that reserve, the results can be very powerful when multiplied over several hundred or several thousand employees.

Another way of describing this phenomenon is the "fifth note." When the four voices of a barbershop quartet are balanced and in perfect harmony, it's possible to hear a fifth note that no one is singing. A scientist would explain that the synchrony of the waveforms melds the four voices into a unified sound while simultaneously creating the perception of a fifth voice. But to the rest of us, it is literally a case where the whole is greater than the sum of its parts.

When the proper conditions are in place to support a culture of respect and dignity, what I like to call the Good Work Place, people will respond in kind and put forth the discretionary effort that makes for superior performance. The question, of course, is how do we inspire them? How can we appeal to their higher selves? It starts with treating people like the talent and valuable resource we hired them to be, trusting in their skills and judgments, believing that they know what to do and letting them do it. And by providing the resources and conditions that enable rather than thwart their efforts.

The people who contributed to this book share my convictions, and they have developed some new and exciting ideas to reshape the environment, to inspire the best in their people. They understand that there is much to be gained by marketing to employees. After all, they are more the company's "brand" than any slogan or advertising campaign. A mix of HR discipline and some Marketing savvy can go a long way to engage employees and align their efforts with the company's goals. That's the power of the partnership that Will and I felt when we worked together at Xerox. And it was our shared experience that inspired us to produce this book. As Libby Sartain so aptly put it, "CHROs and CMOs should be best buddies in the organization."

Reading this book will help you discover:

- How the CHRO and Global Marketing Officer of a *Fortune* 150 company forged a long-term partnership for the benefit of not only employees, but also the bottom line.

- Why the former CHRO at two major corporations believes that the key to success in the marketplace lies in putting employees first—and developing the internal brand *before* the external brand.

- How a high-tech company equipped all its employees, not just the engineers, to understand the intricacies of new products and serve as effective brand ambassadors.

- Why the CHRO of a major financial services firm sees a strong employer brand as the key to attracting and retaining the best talent.

- Why the CEO of the world leader in workforce solutions, the CHRO at a *Fortune* 150 company and a former head of OD all believe that strategic workforce planning is a prerequisite for CHROs to earn a seat at the table.

- How the CEO of a small startup engaged the entire staff in creating the company's brand.

- Why investing in the quality of a company's managers has a multiplier effect.

My partner, Will, and I hope that the answers to these questions and the experiences of the contributors to our book will spark some ideas and the impetus to try them in your company. We wish you success.

chapter one | **Branding a Destination Employer**

Lisa Buckingham
EVP, Chief Human Resources Officer,
Brand & Enterprise Communications,
Lincoln Financial Group

Based in the Philadelphia region, Lincoln Financial Group offers annuities; life, group life, disability and dental insurance; retirement plan services; savings plans; and comprehensive financial planning and advisory services. Lincoln is known for innovation in life insurance and annuity products, and it enjoys a leadership position among United States companies for life and annuities sales. Lincoln has more than 8,500 direct employees as well as approximately 8,100 independent financial planners who market its products. Lisa Buckingham joined Lincoln in 2008 as Chief Human Resources Officer. Since November 2010, she has also been responsible for Brand and Enterprise Communications.

Lisa Buckingham believes that talent is critical to the success of any organization. When she joined Lincoln, Lisa set a goal to make the company the destination employer for the best and brightest in financial services—to attract and then grow them through mentoring and development assignments. As Lisa explained, "That means we have a talent development framework, along with a calibrated performance management and performance review process. Even for early-stage employees, we work hard to recruit, attract and then invest in their development."

5

Lisa's goal required a two-pronged approach. The first step was to develop an employer brand that supported the goal of making Lincoln a destination employer. The follow-up required ensuring that communications and HR processes, especially those related to talent, were consistent with the goal and employer brand.

Creating an Employer Brand

Lisa engaged Will Ruch and the Versant team to create an employer brand for Lincoln. Working together, they surveyed employees and conducted focus groups to find out what was important to employees, what motivated them to stay. They also gathered input from the leaders of Lincoln's major businesses. Analyzing large sets of both quantitative and qualitative data, they distilled the emergent themes into three elements that became the basis of Lincoln's employer brand. It's useful to think in terms of Libby Sartain's (see page 38) definition of employer brand as "the promise an organization makes to the people who do work for it."

Meaningful Work   Dedicated People   Confident Future

Lincoln launched its employer brand in 2010 with a comprehensive communications campaign. Concurrently, Lisa and her team strengthened and, in some cases, re-engineered critical HR processes to make Lincoln a destination employer.

Attracting Talent

Talent starts with hiring. "Beginning in 2010, we worked on a total overhaul of our service delivery model in the talent acquisition area. We interviewed stakeholders across all of Lincoln's businesses— the people who came through our recruiting process and the business hiring managers. We asked them a series of questions:

- What's working? And what isn't?
- Are we going to the right sources for talent?
- How successful are we at hiring the best and brightest?

"We worked closely with our business leaders on reshaping the whole model. In addition, we said our employer brand needs to be alive and well in our recruitment materials, in what we say and how we act with candidates. From the minute a candidate touches Lincoln—from our Web site, from an ad on Monster or Hot Jobs— we're trying to create true brand consistency. We want them to feel and understand our employer brand when they're going through the candidate experience. We've taken a significant amount of time, resources and energy to build our employer brand. We have to live our brand. If we bring in candidates and they don't feel that, then we've missed a major opportunity."

Talent must be applied to the needs of the business. "Before the beginning of each year, we sit down with the business leaders to talk about what they see as the emerging skills and the talent gaps. The leadership team spends a great deal of time in those conversations. It's a little about workforce planning, but it's more looking inside, looking at our skill sets and performance reviews to identify any trends. Do we need to create development plans to address those trends? Or customize programs if we see a skills gap?"

Rewarding Performance

Talented, high-performing employees want to be recognized for their contributions. Like many organizations, Lincoln uses a five-point scale in its performance evaluations. When Lisa arrived, the actual ratings reflected a Lake Woebegone philosophy, where everyone is above average, rather than pay for performance. "There were more fours and fives throughout the organization, even though we weren't hitting all our objectives or creating the total shareholder return that we needed to."

HR and Marketing are becoming disciplines with a strategic voice.

Everyone seemed to understand that a two rating is unsatisfactory and comes with counsel on areas for improvement. As Lisa explained, "The more difficult task was getting managers to understand that three actually represents solid performance. We educated managers on the need for consistency across the organization."

The downturn in 2008 and 2009 was a double-edged sword. "The market crisis was really a reset for our employees and managers," Lisa said. "We had to make very hard decisions when there were layoffs. Managers had to make sure they were keeping high performers, which underscored the need for consistency across the organization. If there were twos, we moved them out. But that made it even more difficult in 2010."

Lisa concedes that creating a true pay-for-performance culture hasn't been easy, but there were clear success factors. "We've had the absolute support of our compensation committee and our CEO. The tone from the top has been there since we started, and that made a big difference." And then there was what Lisa calls "extreme strategic communications at all levels."

In 2010, the employee engagement survey yielded negative feedback from employees who didn't understand how their bonuses worked. With a large percentage on bonus plans—not unusual in the financial services sector—it was a big problem. "We realized that we needed to do a better job of communicating with employees, early and up front, about how our incentive plans work. That was a big learning for us. Now we're communicating on almost a monthly basis."

Managers also needed help. "Training our managers to have those tough performance discussions was critical. They have to have the courage to be direct. They need to set appropriate goals up front and be consistent with their feedback throughout the year. That helps employees understand how pay for performance works. And there should be no surprises. On bonus day, if somebody who was expecting a bonus doesn't get one, then we have failed as leaders."

It took work and a lot of HR people doing one-on-one coaching sessions with managers, but it's succeeding. Managers are differentiating to give greater rewards to top performers.

No Surprises

Lisa doesn't want any Lincoln employee to get an unpleasant surprise on bonus day. Likewise, "What comes out of the HR organization is never a surprise for the businesses. There's a lot of discussion, and we make sure that every dollar we're investing is focused on something that will have a strong business outcome."

Nor are there any surprises in what Lisa and her team measure. "We've built a strategic HR measurement dashboard that we developed through the voice of the customer. We asked our business unit leaders and their CFOs, 'What measures are worthwhile to you?' Our dashboard covers talent pipelines, performance management, pay for performance as well as diversity and inclusion. And to ensure that we're responding to what our employees asked for, we also track the results of our employee engagement surveys."

A Road Map to a Confident Future

Lincoln's career planning and development framework falls squarely under the employer brand umbrella. Feedback from recent employee engagement surveys confirmed that employees want to stay and grow at Lincoln. But they were looking for more career development opportunities. "So we put a lot of work into defining career ladders within functions and finding ways to have people move across the organization into different areas," said Lisa. "We don't want our employees going anywhere else. We've made an investment in them, to have long-term, high-performing employees who live our brand every day."

One of the opportunities available to senior-level Lincoln employees is the Wharton Development Program. Created in conjunction with faculty from the University of Pennsylvania's Wharton School, it's customized specifically for Lincoln. During the past two years, more than 100 executives have completed the program.

The Wharton collaboration also benefits employees below the executive level. "We have Wharton professors come on site to do classroom programs with similar content for every level of employee. We're trying to take it as deep as we can," said Lisa. "In addition, we're continuously developing online content to ensure that our leadership and emerging leadership programs have the same vocabulary, the same principles. And that helps us measure and calibrate performance very consistently across the organization because we're measuring against our leadership expectations, the framework for all our development programs."

Expanding the Employer Brand

Lisa acknowledged that developing the Lincoln employer brand required a deep partnership across the company—and a lot of hard work. "It hasn't always been the easiest journey. But once we got everybody on the same page, we all agreed how important employer brand is and how it touches so many facets of the organization. We recognized that there needs to be a consistency in what we're saying and what our values are. It's been powerful and a lot of fun."

Beginning in November 2010, Lisa became responsible for Corporate Marketing, Enterprise Communications and Brand, in addition to HR. And she is making the most of this convergence. For example, HR and the Brand organization are working together to increase Lincoln's focus on corporate social responsibility. "We have a foundation that donates $10 million a year to communities around the country, focused on health, human services, the arts and education. We're taking the foundation to the next level and ensuring that it's living our employer brand. We're taking an opportunity to promote externally, again from inside out, what we're doing in philanthropy and volunteerism. We've asked our people, 'Who sits on a nonprofit board? What are you doing in your community?' And we're now doing lots of spotlights on those employees. That's effective from a recruiting perspective because it connects out in the marketplace as well."

Lisa has also engaged employees in the company's external brand. Lincoln launched a new marketing campaign in November 2011. "We tested the campaign with customers in three different markets and, of course, with the senior leadership team. But we also wanted our new brand to resonate with our employees, one they could get behind and feel part of. We have to think about how to ignite our external brand across the organization with our employees. We want to develop even deeper brand ambassadors. When we shared the new campaign with groups of employees, they were really excited and even emotional. That was extremely gratifying."

Differentiating Lincoln as a Good Place to Work

Lisa understands that a strong culture can make a financial services company a more attractive employer. "Some competitor organizations have a nuts-and-bolts culture: 'This is your job. Keep doing it well and you can stay here.' Lincoln is using the voice of the employee in developing and refining our employer brand. We take career development very seriously. We're listening to our employees. And we're trying to introduce innovation so that we're ahead of the game."

As an example of the latter, Lisa talked about "Shape up, Lincoln," a health and wellness strategy introduced in 2008. "We were creating a shared responsibility with our workforce. Healthcare costs today are extraordinarily high for every organization. If we have a healthier workforce, then hopefully our experience ratings will go down and we'll have a less expensive premium increase."

The initial result was impressive. "We had 89 percent of our workforce sign up for the walking program. Everyone who joined got a pedometer. It almost became a badge of honor; you'd see people wearing them on their belts. We had departments and buildings competing with each other. It's created this unbelievable culture of healthy competition. We're trying to respond to what our employees have asked for, and we're asking them to live their lives a little bit differently and more healthy. We didn't recognize how powerful this could be."

The 2009 employee engagement confirmed that all of HR's efforts, around communications, development and innovation, were paying off. Against the financial services benchmark of 35 percent of employees being "highly engaged," Lincoln's score was 53 percent—in the midst of a market crisis. "We're listening to our employees; we're having fun with them. We're asking them to work hard, asking them to be ambassadors of this organization. We partner with them, and we get so much in return from them."

Disciplines, not Functions

In closing, Lisa reflected on the areas traditionally regarded as staff functions. "I believe that Human Resources, Marketing and Communications are evolving to be more like disciplines rather than functions. And disciplines with a strategic voice. When we provide the appropriate strategic support to the business, it's absolutely a home run. Today, effective leaders don't look at HR or Marketing as expensive overhead. Our CEO certainly uses this organization as a strategic partner."

Ask the Partners

Q: In HR, there are things that you can't immediately measure. How do you keep the investment momentum up? How do you keep the support going? From my perspective, I've learned to partner with the leadership team and the businesses to ensure that they see value in these things. Do you have advice on how to keep things alive when we're now actually down to counting nickels and dimes? Every organization is. How do HR people convince their leadership to continue to invest when you can't measure something immediately?

A: Research supports the fact that levels of employee engagement are correlated to customer loyalty. Employee engagement can be measured and monitored, as can customer loyalties and financial success. What we know about employee engagement is that employees want to see themselves in the picture, that is, have an impact; make a difference. They want to be a part of the organization's growth strategy *because the company invests in them.* Development, reward and recognition and good workplace are all investments that can and should be correlated to employee engagement and therefore to customer loyalty and finally to business success.

When employee behaviors tie to (and hopefully exceed) customer expectations, the organization creates a competitive advantage that drives growth. This feedback will help leaders see how your internal branding creates a better customer relationship, a stronger connection to the customer experience that is tied into the values and quality of service that customers expect from your company.

chapter two | **Making it Happen at the Restaurant**

Rich Floersch — *CHRO, McDonald's Corporation*
Dean Barrett — *Global Marketing Officer, McDonald's Corporation*

Rich Floersch is the Chief Human Resource Officer, and Dean Barrett is the Global Marketing Officer at McDonald's Corporation. For the past eight years, they have collaborated on employer branding and marketing efforts focused on employees at the restaurant level. McDonald's, headquartered in Oak Brook, Illinois, has 1.8 million employees worldwide. The company manages, either directly or through a network of franchisees, more than 33,000 restaurants in 119 countries. Globally, McDonald's has more than 25 million "alumni" who can list the company on their résumés.

In the next 24 hours, 68 million people will walk into or drive up to a McDonald's restaurant. For CHRO Rich Floersch and GMO Dean Barrett, that's 68 million opportunities for a McDonald's employee to create a great customer experience. That's just one of many things they agree on, based on years of successful collaboration. In fact, when we invited Rich to participate in this book, he said yes—as long as he and Dean could do it together. That was an offer we couldn't refuse.

Right from the Beginning

Rich's arrival as McDonald's CHRO eight years ago coincided with a number of changes at the company. There was a new leadership team in place, and McDonald's had just launched its first global marketing campaign ("I'm lovin' it," which is still around today). That campaign was the impetus for Rich and Dean to collaborate. "We saw a business reason for HR and Marketing to work together. We just knew that we were going to end up with better ideas," Rich said.

They started working on an employer branding campaign, spotlighting the talent that had worked at McDonald's. As Rich explained, "There are fabulous skills that people can get working at McDonald's that they can leverage either inside the company or outside. We teamed up on that campaign, highlighting people like former White House Chief of Staff Andrew Card, the athlete Carl Lewis and the actress Sharon Stone. That project jump-started the notion that we've got to get as much into our employment brand as we do our marketing campaign, because the two of them intersect."

"I'm a Marketing person," Dean said, "but I happen to believe that our largest and most important asset at McDonald's is our people. It's not our products; it's not our creative. It's not a lot of other things that Marketing people talk about. The success of our brand is based on the people who serve our customers. It's impossible to talk about growth drivers without talking about the people who are going to make it happen. They are the brand ambassadors on the front line. Not having a connection between Marketing and HR, on really showcasing our biggest and most important asset, would be a mistake for any brand."

McDonald's has a saying that perfectly captures Dean and Rich's position: "It doesn't happen until it happens at the restaurant." That's their mantra. Rich, who's spent so much time working with Dean that he could easily be mistaken for a Marketing guy, said,

"Advertising is important. New products are important. And we've found that reimaging our restaurants is important. But at the end of the day, that customer experience, the interaction the customer has with our employees is going to define how they feel about the brand more than anything else. The most important, the most credible expression of the brand is our employees at the restaurant level."

Then Dean started sounding like the HR half of the pair. "It happens at the restaurant because of the people running and working in our restaurants. The interaction with customers is what makes the brand different. Marketing and HR, working together, can capture ways to make the brand difference unique. We want to come up with ways to energize those people on a daily basis."

The most important, the most credible expression of the brand is our employees at the restaurant level.

Giving Employees Bragging Rights

One of the ways Rich and Dean energize people is around bragging rights. "People want to brag about who they work for," Rich said. "Bragging rights come down to things they know they're getting at a company that they have a pretty good feel people at other companies aren't getting. We do segmentation and differentiation on the marketing side; there's no reason why we can't differentiate our employment brand. These are the kind of high-impact, 'only at

McDonald's' kinds of experiences, exclusive to McDonald's. Because we're such a big brand, we see great opportunities to be able to collaborate and leverage this brand. And offer people things that are just outstanding experiences, once in a lifetime."

Voice of McDonald's

Dean picked up the thread to talk about one of those experiences. "'Voice of McDonald's' is all about showcasing and energizing the fantastic people who work for the company. It rivals 'American Idol' in terms of the talent."

In fact, the program follows a similar model. It's a biennial singing competition open to all McDonald's restaurant employees worldwide. Much of the publicity for the program is distributed electronically and through social media platforms. For 2012, more than 20,000 employees have entered. Each of the four major geographies—North America, Latin America, Europe and Asia-Pacific/Middle East & Africa—sends its four finalists to the company's convention. "We bring in about 15,000 people from around the world, our franchisees, our suppliers and McDonald's people. Our semifinalists perform in front of the convention audience. The winner gets a $25,000 prize, along with the potential for a recording contract and to be part of a McDonald's commercial. It's just a great way for us to be able to say we've got talent throughout our system, and we want to give people this once-in-a-lifetime opportunity that only McDonald's can offer," said Dean.

At the 2010 convention, singer/songwriter Richard Marx was one of the judges responsible for whittling down the semifinalists to the final three who perform on the last day, when the winner is selected. Rich recalled what Richard said to the finalists. "To be honest with you, I thought this was going to be a little bit of a talent contest where I'd see maybe one or two people who were good, and I'd have to be polite about everybody else. But you are, pound for pound, better than the 'American Idol' people." Rich said, "It was just terrific to hear that. The opportunity it gives the participants, the confidence they get, can be life changing." To find out more about the Voice of McDonald's, go to http://voiceofmcdonalds.com/

Olympic Champion Crew

McDonald's has been an Olympic sponsor since 1976. As part of that sponsorship for the 2012 Games in London, the company will be setting up restaurants in the Olympic Village, the media center and other venues. "Dean and I do our Olympic Champion Crew together. We send our top performing managers to run these restaurants. And we staff them both locally and globally," said Rich. "We're going to have upward of 100 people from around the world flying in. They'll work four-hour shifts at our restaurants and stay in a five-star hotel, getting the wonderful experience of going to London and the Olympic Games."

"Talk about an experience of a lifetime," said Dean. "You're working inside the Olympic Village, dealing with 15,000 of the best athletes from around the world; that is a tremendous brand experience. And the athletes love it. Crew members wear buttons that identify which languages they speak, so the athletes can find someone from their home country."

In fact, the company's role at the Olympics extends beyond its Champion Crew. The London Organising Committee of the Olympic Games and Paralympic Games (LOCOG) approached McDonald's UK with a request. As Dean explained, "We are probably one of the biggest and best trainers in the UK today, in terms of our approach and learning strategies. The committee asked us to take on the responsibility for training all 70,000 volunteers who will be working at the Games. Because of our expertise and our people skills, McDonald's people will be training those volunteers in addition to our Champion Crew."

It Takes a Team

Rich and Dean represent one example of successful teamwork. Rich described McDonald's as a team-based environment and commented that, "If you're not effective operating in teams at McDonald's, you're probably not going to be very successful."

About two years ago, the two men expanded their team to a Global People Board, adding the heads of Operations and IT. They recognized that those two functions played a critical role in enabling restaurant managers to be successful and for their crews to feel like they're working for a contemporary company. The board's role is to accelerate innovation across the company.

One of the initiatives the board is looking to scale is "Our Lounge," an application developed by the McDonald's UK HR group. It's an employee communications portal that provides a combination of company information and popular content. Using this portal, employees can do their own schedules online, eliminating the need for the manager to sift through 60 different employees' preferences. Employees can access e-learning content and check last night's football (or soccer, as it's known in the United States) scores. The proof of a successful portal: 40,000 former McDonald's employees continue to use it. That's not surprising, since "Our Lounge" plays to all three "F" factors that topped employees' lists about why they liked working at McDonald's (see sidebar, page 23).

Bragging Rights for the Company

Working to make sure that employees have bragging rights about McDonald's has created some bragging rights for the company itself. In October 2011, McDonald's made the inaugural "Best Global Companies to Work for" list. "We were fortunate enough to be recognized as No. 8," Rich said. "We're right in there with Google and Microsoft." The article in *Fortune* quoted a McDonald's employee who said, "This company cares about people— developing them, training them and giving them the tools to do their job confidently and effectively. There's a great training system, and also a clear focus of where we are and where we are going." Testimonials don't get much better than that.

And on the very day of our interview, Rich learned that McDonald's had also made the 2011 "Top Companies for Leaders" list, also in the No. 8 position on the global list, and No. 5 on the North American list. Again, McDonald's is in good company, with IBM, Procter & Gamble and General Mills. The kudos extend to the brand as well. Dean reported, "Our brand is No. 6 in the Interbrand survey of the leading brands of the world for the value of the brand. And we're not happy with No. 6. We want to be No. 1."

Dean and Rich aren't content to rest on these accolades. "The one thing that is a strong value here is continuous learning and development," Rich said. "The last thing we ever want to do is feel we've cracked the code on any of this, because once you do, that's the first day you start to go down. There's just so much more that we can get better at. We know there are plenty of opportunities for us to collaborate, between Marketing and HR. There's great energy here for us to keep getting better together."

Dean agreed. "We will continue to do everything we can, working cross-functionally across our company to continue to improve. But improvement is only meaningful if it makes a difference for our customers and employees. It's not about winning a survey here or there; it's about the fact that the survey reinforces that we're doing the right things."

The Three F's

"When we asked our employees about what they loved about working at McDonald's, HR worked with Dean's group and boiled it down to the three F's," Rich said.

"**Family and friends**: People love that sense of community in the restaurant. And using social media, you could now do this across all restaurants in a market."

"**Flexibility**: About their work hours and working different jobs within the restaurant."

"And the one we're so pleased to see make the list, **Future**: That's development opportunities and career growth."

The last is borne out by some hard statistics. Forty percent of McDonald's top 50 executives started out working in a restaurant. The vast majority of the company's franchisees started out that way as well.

Ask the Partners

Q: How are companies' HR and Marketing leaders jointly approaching social media?

A: Your question anticipates the first part of our response, that this is an area for HR and Marketing to collaborate. We recommend starting by looking at how your company uses social media externally, with customers, potential employees and the general public. For example, some companies use channels like Facebook as a way to keep tabs on customer satisfaction levels, an early warning system for in-store issues that need to be addressed or even as a recruitment tool. The company's use of social media with external audiences provides the context for internal use; they should be consistent. For example, a company that makes extensive use of social media is likely to have a savvy employee population that is already actively engaged with Facebook, Twitter and other channels.

If your company doesn't already have a policy on employees' use of social media, this is a perfect opportunity for HR and Marketing to work together to generate positive, constructive thinking around effective use of these growing channels. Both could increase their stock within the company by being forward thinking and enabling responsible use. Employees need—and in many cases want—appropriate guidelines to follow. A company's social media policy should be part of and in keeping with its ethics policy.

chapter three | **Engaging Talent in the Human Age**

Jeff Joerres
Chairman & CEO, ManpowerGroup

ManpowerGroup is the world leader in innovative workforce solutions that enable clients to achieve business goals and improve their competitiveness. A Fortune 150 company with more than 60 years of experience, ManpowerGroup operates 4,000 offices in 80 countries. On any given day, ManpowerGroup has 600,000 employees working for customers around the globe, in addition to 30,000 people who work directly for the company. Jeff Joerres was appointed President and CEO in 1999; he has been Chairman and CEO since May 2001. ManpowerGroup is a strategic partner of the World Economic Forum, and in January 2011, Jeff introduced ManpowerGroup's leading-edge thinking on "The Human Age."

As CEO of ManpowerGroup, Jeff Joerres is, quite literally, in the talent business. He spends a lot of time thinking about talent, to the point that he has achieved preeminence as a thought leader. He arguably knows more about talent than anyone else in the world.

Matching Clients and Talents

ManpowerGroup is in the business of matching the skills of candidates to the talent requirements of their clients. Ultimately, it's a relationship built on trust. Clients trust that ManpowerGroup can provide people with the right skills. And candidates trust that

ManpowerGroup will match them with the right company, in terms of both skills and culture.

ManpowerGroup's Candidate Experience is critical to successful matches. "The match is an integral part of what we do," said Jeff. "We actually have a complete process, from before the person walks in the door to after they become an employee. We call that the Candidate Experience. The predictability of that system, which was put in every office in every country, is a major part of how we can create a strong process that actually makes a better match. As a result, that employee is much more valuable to our client."

And there are legions of candidates. In any given year, ManpowerGroup interviews 10 million to 12 million people, which makes for a lot of brand-defined encounters. "That's really where we spend a lot of the time. That candidate trust, that individual trust, we take very seriously when a person comes into our office, either electronically or physically, looking for a job. It's one of the advantages of being in business as long as we are and have been, and also how seriously we take the task at hand."

Everything about the Candidate Experience matters—the readiness before someone comes into the office, the questions, the follow-up, the diligence to find the person a job. "All of those things that we have trained for become part of that trust factor," said Jeff. Although labor laws vary from country to country, Jeff says that "at the core, you could walk into a ManpowerGroup office in Kyoto or Milwaukee and have the same candidate experience, and our staff would be following the same process."

It was actually the 2008-09 downturn that enabled ManpowerGroup to launch the Candidate Experience and fine-tune its processes. The recession was the worst that ManpowerGroup has experienced. It was very much a labor downturn, and it was global; every country was hit at virtually the same time. ManpowerGroup took advantage of the slowdown in their offices. "We took a hard look at ourselves, and we actually invested in technology. We introduced the Candidate Experience and new releases of training. As a result, we were able to take 5 percent market share every quarter during the first 18 months of the upside. As an organization, we're stronger because of what we went through; we're able to handle faster, more abrupt movements. It's not just change in the labor market, but the speed of change. There are no glide paths, up or down, anymore."

And that agility is good news for ManpowerGroup's clients. In these uncertain times, more companies are shifting the talent burden from their shoulders to ManpowerGroup's. Recruiting is just one example. "Our clients have seen the requirement for agility, flexibility and for someone who is the 'real professional' doing the recruitment in a scientific way."

In the past, when companies decided to hire, they would have to hire ten recruiters before each recruiter could hire ten people a month. "Now they just say, 'We need 25 new people this month,' and we have the recruiters to do that. In the old vernacular, that would be outsourcing. But it's really a partnership that goes much deeper," Jeff said. "We do some of the recruiting; they do some of the recruiting. But there's no doubt they have shifted much of the expertise and burden to us, because they see us being able to do it better and faster."

Jeff says that finding talent, even with high unemployment, is getting more difficult. "A major reason is that companies are making the job mean more, putting more content into the job, which increases the capabilities that are required. The result is often a talent mismatch," said Jeff. "We're a big part of solving it, but it puts a lot of stress on our organization. If I could fill all my open orders, we'd be in great shape. We're having a hard time finding people."

Rapidly changing business conditions, an increasing number of talent mismatches and the need for flexibility and agility are all hallmarks of what ManpowerGroup has identified as the Human Age.

The Human Age*

Jeff uses the *Human Age* to describe the new era in which we now live. Early eras were defined first by the raw materials that characterized them—stone, bronze and iron. Subsequent eras were named for the domains that technology enabled people to master—industry, space and information. We have now entered the Human Age, named for the element that will be the greatest catalyst for change and innovation: human potential. According to Jeff, optimizing human potential will be the single most important determinant for businesses to succeed and grow.

* For more on Jeff Joerres' thinking on The Human Age, visit
   http://manpowergroup.com/humanage/

The Human Age is characterized by great transformation, radical changes and new developments. Global economic and demographic forces have strained existing models to the breaking point. To succeed, or even survive, companies will have to develop new business models and people practices, and evolve their talent strategies and structures.

ManpowerGroup is no exception. "We're widening the aperture of what's required of our people. We're trying to evolve to be a very fast, agile, collaborative organization. That takes a lot of work and a lot of behavior changing," said Jeff. "We're implementing new training programs, different criteria for success and a new leadership model based on collaboration. We try to be as clear as possible, because it gives our people a better chance to succeed."

Despite the stress and uncertainty, Jeff is optimistic. He believes that the pressure to do more with less through the recession has made employers realize the true power of human potential. "With the right people in the right place at the right time, organizations can achieve all they did before, and more," said Jeff. "Employers need to ensure that they have the right people practices in place to attract, retain and unleash the inner human potential of the right people to succeed in the Human Age."

In the past, companies needed access to capital to fuel their growth. Jeff sees human potential ultimately replacing capital as the new dominant resource. Or as he puts it, "Capitalism is evolving into talentism."

Talent in the Human Age

Talent in the Human Age is less about the rare individual with esoteric skills than it is about people with the right skills at the right time, people who continuously learn and update their skills. "Individuals who are lifelong learners, explorers, people with intellectual curiosity—that's what we're looking for. We can place them faster, we can find them jobs faster. And they tend to grow with an organization, even though the organization may be completely different from what it was just three or four years ago. Lifelong learners have the ability to grow with organizations and change with them," said Jeff.

This is the time for HR to step up
and ensure their company has
the talent it needs to win.

People who are motivated by greater responsibility and opportunities for career growth, people who are comfortable working collaboratively with their teams will be in greater demand. These candidates, in turn, will become more assertive about when and where they want to work. And that requires new ways of sourcing, developing and retaining talent in a world where the pace of change is accelerating. As an example, companies will have to adapt their recruiting and development strategies to take individual needs and preferences into consideration.

One of Jeff's biggest concerns is structural, long-term unemployment, both in the United States and worldwide. "If you've been out of work for two years, the game has changed on you dramatically. That's two, three generations of work life."

In the Human Age, talent means being open to new things, having the willingness to change and grow. Companies that inspire, that enable the innovation of their people to bubble up are the ones that are going to succeed. "Inspiring now is much more important and much more difficult because of all the noise levels around that inspiration. To be able to create your own environment as a company, an environment that has energy and lifelong learning and development all incorporated into one, those are going to be the winners," said Jeff.

The Challenges for HR: Engagement and Workforce Planning

As the stewards of talent, HR organizations have a significant role to play in the Human Age in two major areas: engagement and workforce planning.

Understanding how to unleash human potential is not a one-size-fits-all approach; it requires employers to engage with their people on a human level. In fact, Jeff uses the expression "one size fits one"; it needs to be that personal. In the Human Age, engagement has to be more open, more transparent, much more of a conversation. "Technology and the growth of social media have led to a new level of transparency and given us the ability to have a human-to-human conversation with almost everyone."

As Jeff explains, "Engagement isn't: 'You're going to work here and I'm going to continue to develop you. You'll continue to get 3 percent raises for the rest of your life, so you should be happy.' In the past, I think there was a lot of reliance on that for engagement. But the rules have changed dramatically. The companies started it, and the individuals have accelerated it. So it's the kind of conversations you have, the implicit and explicit promises that you make to the individuals—about their growth and the pace at which they can grow, about their contribution and about their feeling of pride to their contribution."

Learning and development are clearly part of the equation, but in a different way. "It's not sending somebody off for six months to a program or two weeks to a class, though some of that still exists and should exist. A lot of it is increasing engagement through increased exposure to different things within an organization. And you grow talent at the same time you get work done," Jeff said. "You need to do it without pushing the burnout factor too far, and actually feeling the energy of what that means to an individual. That, all connected to 'I am part of the company's success' is what we firmly believe drives engagement at the end of the day."

Of course, successful engagement requires having the right employees in place. Talent mismatch—the inability to find the right skills in the right place at the right time—is a looming threat for all employers. If talent mismatch is the symptom, then poor workforce planning—or even the complete lack of it—is the underlying problem.

Working for Two Brands

If the feeling that "I am part of the company's success" is the key driver of employee engagement, what about employees who work for two brands? An increasing percentage of the labor force now consists of people who work *for* one employer and *at* another. For many companies, this is the new reality. For ManpowerGroup, it's their history and inherent in their business model. The people they deploy to customer sites are legally ManpowerGroup's employees in every country in which they operate.

So how does ManpowerGroup help their people feel like they contribute to the success of both companies? It starts with the matching process. "When we put somebody into a client location, we talk about how they're there to help them win, and the fit's a big part of it." And so is engaging them in an ongoing conversation. "We're using technology to communicate and connect with our employees. It has its challenges, with 600,000 people speaking multiple languages." The frequency of those communications depends on the length of the assignment and the level of the individual. In many cases, it's as often as once a week. Finally, it's providing the employees opportunities to learn and develop. ManpowerGroup offers training and, more important, valuable on-the-job learning experience.

"We're getting better at helping people understand the value of their contribution to both companies, but there's room for improvement," Jeff acknowledged.

Like Jay Spach (see page 116), Jeff is a strong proponent of serious, strategic workforce planning. He recommends that employers ask themselves whether their current workforce strategies support their plans for long-term growth in a changing environment. "Given how dramatically the world has changed, and the fact that the speed of change is accelerating," Jeff said, "the answer is almost certainly 'No.'"

Prompted by the recession, companies have focused on reducing cost to improve productivity. Wide-scale reductions in force resulted in high, seemingly intractable unemployment. In spite of high unemployment, ManpowerGroup's sixth annual Talent Shortage Survey showed that 34 percent of employers worldwide reported that they couldn't fill key positions.

To be effective, a company's workforce strategy must have the ability "to generate the talent needed to achieve the CEO's vision and long-term goals of the business," said Jeff. "HR leaders are the essential link in aligning workforce strategy to business strategy. HR needs not only to help the business identify the gaps between their business strategy and workforce strategy, but they also need to design a road map for success."

In Jeff's view, a robust and well-documented workforce strategy:

- Reflects a longer term, more comprehensive focus than an annual talent plan,
- Focuses on the work models that will produce the best results for the organization,
- Identifies the people practices that need to be updated,
- Includes an outside-in view on talent sources, and
- Differentiates between the required skills the organization can build vs. those it must buy.

Aligning workforce strategy to the business strategy is not a "once and done" activity, but an iterative, ongoing process. "It's the HR leader's role to facilitate this process with leadership," said Jeff. To be effective, that process must encompass both external forces (competition, demographic trends) and internal variables (current workforce demographics). "The organizations that get this right will have the competitive edge. This is the time for HR to step up and lead the way to ensure their company has the talent it needs to win."

Looking Ahead

The Human Age presentation at Davos garnered Jeff and ManpowerGroup a bounty of favorable press coverage and recognition. For ManpowerGroup employees, it's become a source of pride that their company has the thought leadership to be taking a big stand like this.

For Jeff, the Human Age is not an ad slogan; it's a way of thinking, a way of doing business. Going forward, Jeff plans to expand it, bringing it to life in various countries and building on it. "We have already felt the cumulative effect of getting this right and staying on message, working really hard on adding proof points. And you get more aha moments as a result of it," Jeff said.

And that's a good thing. Clients, and even governments, are looking at using ManpowerGroup more and more to help them deal with the realities they're facing. "That puts pressure on us to have better systems, better people and better processes," said Jeff. "That's what we'll continue to work on. What is really good right now will not be really good a year from now. You've got to keep running and leaning forward."

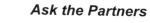

Ask the Partners

Q: I'd like to understand better how governments can stay in step with businesses, when governments are local and businesses are global. Businesses move fast, and governments move slow. And yet, both need each other. So how does that get reconciled?

A: Governments are composed of people, both elected officials and employees who are charged with business success or champion business interests. Keep in active touch to assure that your organization's interests and issues are understood and championed. Find groups that share your organization's interests and can advocate for coordinated local, regional, national and international policies and regulations.

Also, most governments source work from the private sector. Consider how the private sector can provide leadership that helps move government forward.

chapter four | **Putting Employees First**

Libby Sartain
Business Advisor and Former VP, EVP-HR, Yahoo! And Southwest Airlines

Libby Sartain served as head of Human Resources at Southwest Airlines and Yahoo! Both companies made the Fortune *"100 Best Companies to Work for in America" list during her tenure. She is also the co-author, along with Mark Schumann, of* Brand from the Inside *(2006) and* Brand for Talent *(2009). Since 2008, Libby has worked as an independent HR advisor and consultant, helping HR and Marketing executives to create and implement successful employer brands. Libby currently serves on the Boards of Directors of Peets Coffee & Tea, Inc. and ManpowerGroup, Inc.*

With a 30-year career in Human Resources, Libby Sartain knows a lot about HR. Along the way, she's learned a lot about Marketing as well. Like others we interviewed for this book, Libby defines *brand* as "what you stand for in the big picture. It's a big idea." To Libby, *brand* is also about the promises you make.

When it comes to brand, Libby sees two sides of a coin. "I look at brand as having two aspects. I look at the external, consumer or corporate brand as one side of branding; and then I look at the internal brand or employer brand as the other side of branding," Libby explained. "When you look at the consumer or the external brand, you're looking for what you stand for as a company and what you stand for as a product. If you look inside, at your internal brand, you're looking at what do you stand for as employer. On the outside, you make a promise to your customers or consumers; it depends on what your business is all about. On the inside, you make a promise to the people who do work for you, whether they're employees or in some other kind of relationship that they perform work for your customers."

internal/employer brand	external/consumer brand
What you stand for as an employer	What you stand for as a company
The promise you make to the people who perform work for you	What you stand for as a product or service
	The promise you make to your customers

The internal brand is a prerequisite for	**>**	**The external brand**

Here's what may come as a surprise to most Marketing people: Libby is adamant that the internal, employer brand must come first. "You have to put the internal customer first—that's the number-one lesson I learned at Southwest Airlines," Libby explained. "If you think that the person who works here is customer No. 1, and the person who buys our goods and services is customer No. 2, and you live that way every day as if it's a way of life, you'll win. The brand on the outside is what you stand for and what you promise to deliver to customers. The brand on the inside is what you deliver to employees so they can deliver on that brand promise to the customers."

To Libby, it's a straightforward case of cause and effect. "When you're branding outside, you come up with what you stand for and what you promise to customers. Then you have to back into it. If you want to make this promise to customers, do you have the right people inside, the right processes, the right infrastructure and the right experience for your people to deliver on that promise outside? The brand from the inside is all about the employer brand. The reason you brand from the inside with an employer brand is so that you can brand from the outside with your consumer brand. What happens on the outside can't happen unless it happens on the inside first."

Marketing departments are beginning to realize the critical role employees play. As Libby explained, "They can create words and feelings and big ideas and concepts, but the company cannot deliver on it unless everyone who works there or touches the customer in some way understands it, is aligned with it, has internalized it or, the best situation, becomes an ambassador for what the company does."

Rich Floersch, the CHRO at McDonald's, and Dean Barrett, his partner and Global Marketing Officer, absolutely get it. They understand that the work they do at headquarters doesn't matter unless front-line employees internalize it. Their mantra is: "It doesn't happen till it happens at the restaurant." (For more on the McDonald's story, see page 16.)

It Takes a Team

When Libby was head of HR at Southwest Airlines, one of her peers was the head of Marketing. The vice president to whom they both reported brought them together and issued a challenge. "When Marketing comes out with their attempt to tell employees how to behave and what to do and how to deliver on the brand promise, it sounds like a Marketing campaign. And employees roll their eyes with skepticism," the VP said. "When HR comes out with it, it sounds like the latest HR program of the month. And if anything, employees are even *more* skeptical. Can the two of you figure out a way to make this brand just a natural way of life for the people who work here?"

CHROs and CMOs should be best buddies in the organization.

That challenge started Libby and her Marketing partner on the road to employer branding. They approached their task by asking themselves a series of questions:

- What if we were marketing the experience of working at Southwest Airlines as if it were a product?
- How would we sell it?
- How would we describe it?
- How would we talk about what it feels like to work here?

For Libby, employer brand encompasses the whole experience of working for an organization. "Each phase and each stage should be treated with the same amount of forethought, planning, process and structure as the customer experience. Nirvana would be if you took every employee experience, every touchpoint, and you branded that experience and you created a consistent experience throughout," Libby said. Right now, she believes that many companies should be focusing on what is probably the most neglected part of the employee life cycle: how to help people depart in a way that helps them feel good about themselves and tell a good story about their experience at the company.

At the time, Libby and her Marketing partner at Southwest Airlines thought that they were the first company to come up with "branding from the inside out" or employer branding. It was an idea whose time had come, however, and they later discovered that other companies had independently started working on the same concept.

Based on her experience at both Southwest and Yahoo!, and working with her co-author Mark Schumann, Libby's perfected an operational definition of *employer brand* that she continues to use in her consulting work:

> How a business builds and packages its identity,
> origins and values, and what it promises to deliver to
> emotionally connect employees so that they, in turn,
> deliver what the business promises to customers.

Libby establishes some prerequisites before agreeing to work with prospective clients or startups. She knows what it takes to build and launch a successful employer brand. "You've got to have HR, Marketing and Corporate Communications, as well as the head of Operations, the individual responsible for customer-facing people. You've got to have them all in the same room, working on it together," Libby said. "It's never going to succeed if they don't have a collaborative effort involving the whole company, including the CEO. If he or she isn't behind doing this, it's not going to happen."

Brand and Talent

The thesis of Libby's second book is that brand and talent are related. "Talent is attracted to the best brands," she explained. "The best brands are going to have the best talent because people who really understand a brand, and a brand that's done a very good job of stating what they stand for, who they are and what they promise to customers, can reach out and appeal to potential recruits. Brand can be a magnet for the talent that will deliver on the brand promise."

In fact, Libby and Mark Schumann set out to write *Brand for Talent* because they thought that a lot of people were approaching brand in the wrong way. "They were saying, 'We need talent. Let's come up with an employer brand to advertise to our potential talent.' What we were saying is that you have to have the internal brand *first*. Before you reach out, you have to know who you are and what you stand for," Libby said. "Once that internal brand is out there, you can use your marketing tools to reach out to the talent segment you want to bring into the company."

Libby pointed out that Gen Y employees, the Millennials, are highly attuned to the concept of brand. Many of them are looking for what she calls a Facebook- or LinkedIn-worthy job—something that will give them "bragging rights" with their friends and at reunions. She goes on to say that "the top talent will not affiliate with a company unless the brand says something about their _own_ brand. They understand that where they work says something about them. There are 20 or 30 companies that maybe have that panache. But other companies should be creating that panache around what it's like to work there."

Some Recommendations

Based on her experiences, Libby has some suggestions for developing talent within the HR function, particularly preparing HR leaders of the future. "We've specialized so much in the last 20 years that we have a lot of very deep subject matter experts in comp or talent management. But to run an HR function, you have to know it all. My advice is to move people across the different specialties throughout their careers." Libby recommends that HR leaders set up a structure that facilitates that kind of movement.

Development isn't limited to HR specialties; HR people should develop skills and knowledge beyond the function. "It's more important than ever that HR people have a business background to do their role," Libby said. She went on the highlight the importance of Marketing. "If you find yourself going into HR, that's another skill you'll need. An HR person is more or less an internal marketing person when it comes to the strategic elements of the job and selling the employer as a place to work."

And for CHROs, Libby offers this Texas-blunt, but effective bit of advice: "I think that chief human resource officers need to attach themselves at the hip with their CMOs, and they should be the best buddies in the organization. In the past, we operated in silos, and we can't do our best work unless we do it together."

Ask the Partners

Q: I think one of the biggest issues out there, when it comes to the work of employer branding, is how do we measure success? Marketing has all kinds of tools where they measure brand valuations, top brand identification—there are several well-accepted tools. And HR doesn't have those tools yet. What are the top employer brands? How do they deliver on that corporate or consumer brand promise?

A: Libby is absolutely right—measuring the success of an employer brand and how well a company manages it is a huge issue. So we consulted with the best expert we could find: Simon Barrow, founder and chairman of the firm that originated the employer branding approach. To share Simon's expertise with the broadest audience, we've dedicated a chapter to his response. It starts on page 54.

chapter five | Looking Through an Economist's Eyes

Carl Steidtmann
Chief Economist & Director of Consumer Research, Deloitte Research

Carl Steidtmann, chief economist and director of Deloitte Research, Consumer Business, is a nationally recognized subject-matter specialist on economic forecasting of retail sales activity, consumer trends, technology and general economic trends. Based in New York, Dr. Steidtmann works with individual clients to assess the impact of economic, demographic, political and technological changes on their business strategies. Dr. Steidtmann has authored or co-authored more than 400 publications on economics, demographics, competition and sociotechnological trends as they relate to business.

Starting with the marketplace, Carl Steidtmann sees a clear need for a connection between HR and Marketing. "I think for many companies, the reputation that they have as an employer will also affect the reputation of the products and services that they deliver. I think that's particularly true of businesses that are professional services businesses. In many cases, their employees _are_ the product. Even in businesses where that's not the case, the quality of the people who are working for the company and the satisfaction that they have in the work that they're doing are key elements for creating a high-performance company. So I think it's a rather obvious merger between Marketing and Human Resources."

47

That merger has potential benefits for both disciplines. "For Human Resources, they can incorporate marketing techniques to communicate the benefit of working for a particular company. But I think there's an advantage for the Marketing department as well. The better press that they get, the better brand reputation they get about the company itself as a place to work will rub off on the products and services that the company is selling."

Despite what Carl sees as an "obvious merger," he says that a lot of HR people haven't made the connection. "In many cases they're internally focused, trying to satisfy the demands of their internal clients, because that's the way their incentives work. The marketplace takes, at best, a back seat. Over the last decade, labor markets have been relatively flat. So whenever you had a need for some skill set, there wasn't much difficulty going out and finding it."

Attracting talent is a function of the company's employer brand.

But for many HR heads, that could be changing. "One of the interesting findings from some recent surveys is that employers are having a hard time finding the people they want. That's particularly true for a lot of manufacturing companies that are looking for people with technical skills. These skills are in short supply, even though the overall labor market is relatively flat. For those businesses where there are shortages, Human Resources will have to be much more externally oriented."

In a competitive marketplace, Carl said, "Attracting talent is a function of the company's employer brand. The reputation they have for people coming into the business, the quality of training that they're going to get, the variability of the work, the opportunities for advancement—all of those will be factors in attracting people."

But keeping them is something of a different matter. "Most of the research points to the first-line manager as the number-one factor contributing to retention. If people like their bosses, if they feel that the manager is supportive of what the employee is doing, that the manager has an interest in the employee as a person—those factors increase retention. Another factor is having people within the company that the employee views as friends."

Carl confirmed what most HR people know about retention. "Having competitive pay and benefits, having work that's interesting—all that's clearly important. But it really is the more social side of the work environment that, over the long run, seems to be the biggest factor that affects retention."

Metrics

Economists like numbers and measurements. We asked Carl for his suggestions on metrics that could help HR demonstrate its value. For new college hires, he proposed a metric that addressed the quality of hires, like the rankings of the schools they attended and their class rankings. Although not perfect, it does provide companies a way to gauge the attractiveness of their employer brand, as perceived by the most sought-after talent.

Retention, said Carl, "is a pretty hard number. The cost of employee turnover is a fairly well-known number. You can look at how long it takes to get somebody up to speed, the associated training cost, the human capital they create—those are all very measurable numbers. By increasing retention, you obviously generate a return on human capital."

Looking Ahead

We asked Carl to share his thoughts on the skills and talent he believes will become more important in the future. "Having a global perspective will become much more important. For most people, that will mean having overseas experience and being able to speak a foreign language. Fluency in Chinese will be quite helpful. Portuguese would be another language, as Brazil becomes a global player. Being multicultural would probably be one of the most important skills, and probably the hardest for Americans to develop. That's the one skill we know employees are going to need. Because the world will continue to get smaller, and the need to manage in different cultures will only grow."

Sourcing changes as well. "Recruitment of talent is going to become much more of a global phenomenon. We're finding that there are very, very talented people who aren't necessarily located in the United States. We see the process of globally integrating organizations to operate on a 24/7 basis is one of the key drivers of productivity improvement. The recruitment process is going to have to reflect the multicultural, global attributes of the organization itself."

Global sourcing has implications for the development of leaders. Carl pointed out that managing employees from other cultures requires a different approach. They may not respond to the same incentives that work for people who grew up in the United States. When things go wrong, they may overreact to even the best-intentioned feedback. So managers will need to learn new coaching skills to inspire the best performance from their teams.

Ask the Partners

Q: To me, there is an issue on how you develop a multicultural organization. In my mind, that's the main challenge that large businesses are going to have going forward: How do you create a cohesive, multicultural organization that has a common vision? Successful organizations have a set of shared values that everybody operates off of that are both well-articulated and well-understood. And yet, how do you achieve that across a multicultural, a diverse platform of people? The real challenge is to have a common set of values across a diverse set of people.

A: Every organization/enterprise is a social body that has its own culture. It changes, morphs and emerges, but at its core are the organization's values. If you try to accommodate every cultural nuance, you wind up with chaos and confusion. Trust that your people want to belong to something bigger than themselves. Make sure your organization fosters a culture of inclusion that invites everyone in to be a part of the enterprise and aligns them with the overarching goals. Be sure to remove barriers to inclusion, especially unintended biases. "Celebrating" how different everyone is, every day and everywhere, simply continues to reinforce boundaries. These are your people, your talent, your link to the customer and your engine for growth. Celebrate what you achieve together.

To reinforce your expectations and remove doubt about expected and acceptable behaviors and decisions, establish an effective code of business conduct and ethics. Then deploy it throughout the company. Keep it relevant by reviewing and refreshing as your marketplace demands.

chapter six | **Evaluating the Impact of Employer Brand Management**

Simon Barrow
Founder and Chairman, People in Business (London)

People in Business (PiB) is the London-based consultancy that originated the Employer Brand approach and now has more than two decades experience in shaping industry thinking on this subject. The firm (owned by TMP Worldwide LLC North America since 2007) works with client organizations to define the qualities that differentiate them as an employer and develop an employee value proposition for current and potential employees. Simon Barrow is the founder and Chairman of PiB and co-author, with Richard Mosley, of The Employer Brand: Bringing the Best of Brand Management to People at Work. *Simon believes that the best employer brands are built from the inside out, starting at the top. He works with leadership teams to develop the attitudes, behaviors and relationships that inspire exceptional performance. PiB also helps clients address the people-related challenges critical for successful mergers and acquisitions.*

When Libby Sartain (see page 38) posed some tough questions about measuring the effectiveness of employer brands, we knew that there was no better source for the answers than Simon Barrow. Since these are important questions of general interest to our readership, we decided to feature Simon's responses in a stand-alone chapter.

Definition of Employer Brand*

We define the *employer brand* as the package of functional, economic and psychological benefits provided by employment and identified with the employing company. The main role of the employer brand is to provide a coherent framework for the management to simplify and focus priorities, increase productivity and improve recruitment, retention and commitment.

*From the original research Simon did with Tim Ambler of the London Business School in 1996

How do you measure the success of Employer Branding?

This is only one of the questions for an employer brand (EB) manager! "Branding" in terms of awareness and attitudes is just a part of how an EB is assessed. There are several long-established ways of measuring brand awareness whether spontaneous or prompted, e.g., the league tables of awareness of among graduates from companies like Ipsos, a global market research company headquartered in Paris; or Universum, a Stockholm-based consulting firm specializing in employer branding.

How you measure the success of an employer brand *overall* is a broader question, and the answers include:

- Greater pulling power. The stronger the EB, the better the performance in attracting less active job seekers, a segment that contains a greater proportion of top-quality candidates. Weak brands attract more active job seekers and fewer top candidates (Corporate Leadership Council).

- Lower recruitment costs. A strong EB lowers the conversion premium when switching organizations. Great people will often jump at the chance of working for such organizations and move for the same money.

- Improved retention. Tesco's EB program achieved a 7 percent reduction in attrition, saving $11 million a year. Tesco, a grocery and general merchandise retailer headquartered in the UK, is the world's third-largest retailer, as measured by revenue. The company has 472,000 employees worldwide.

- Greater engagement. Numerous studies have confirmed the link between employee engagement and improved business performance (Towers Watson, Gallup, Watson Wyatt).

- An employer's own measures including sickness/absence. People are less likely to take sick leave in a top EB. In the UK, there is a marked difference between public sector employees (4.3 percent) versus private sector (2.8 percent) in time lost to sick leave (UK Chartered Institute of Personnel and Development). Furthermore, 37.5 percent of public sector organizations cite "stress" as the biggest cause of long-term absence, versus 11.2 percent in the private sector. The EB of the former must play a significant role.

- Employer research on employee satisfaction and Net Promoter Scores (defined by Bain as those who would recommend the organization to friends and family as a place to work minus those who would not).

- The share prices of *Fortune* 100 Best Places to Work employers outperform the S&P average (Great Place to Work Institute).

- Easier facilitation of M&A and other massive corporate changes. There is no such thing as a merger of equals. When one of the two EBs truly stands out, it makes life a lot easier since everyone wants to work for the stronger player (PiB's experience in 29 M&A transactions).

Numerous studies have confirmed the link between employee engagement and improved business performance.

How do you identify the top employer brands?

I have a list of demanding questions I created for fund managers and analysts (often with little experience outside financial services) which they can use to assess the EB aspects of the companies they study. Here are a few of the dimensions which I believe top employer brands are likely to deliver on:

- The offer to prospective employees is distinctive, compelling and true. (Just try looking at a few career Web sites to see how bland and commonplace most offers are—the result of those responsible being 100 percent on risk avoidance rather than inspiration.)

- The success of alumni—a great EB is a springboard, an academy company.

- The senior HR executive is on the Board of Directors and certainly on the Executive Management Group [Authors' note: In the UK, the senior team—the CEO and his or her direct reports—makes up this team. A publicly traded company also has a Board of Directors elected by shareholders.]

- The last time the company did an M&A, was HR on the initial planning group? A big warning signal if they were not!

- Any employee could tell you the goals of the company.

- What response rate did the last employee survey get?

- How were the results fed back?

- The company's values are unique (very, very few are; most are worthy table stakes like "integrity," which is in 45 percent of all UK FTSE value statements).

- The behaviors driven by the values are embedded in the appraisal system and the fabric of the business.

- The work the company does is regarded as worthwhile and a source of pride.

- The CEO demonstrates a consistent thirst to learn about people-related matters.

- The CEO gets out there, asks questions and listens to the answers.

- The CEO has sufficient self-awareness, demonstrating a balance between self-confidence and humility.

- The company has demonstrated that it can survive the rocks and reefs of commercial life and has usually done better than its competitors.

Does a strong employer brand correlate to delivering on the company's consumer brand promise?

A great EB should shine through every external contact, with customers being the No.1, in addition to suppliers, advisers, potential recruits, alumni, graduate schools, careers officers and the other businesses and joint venture partnerships your company deals with. They should rate you for your people, not just your product or your earnings.

Taking the consumer brand promise specifically, it is worth noting the answers to why customers defect—death, moving, influence of friends, being attracted by a competitor are all factors. But 68 percent of the reasons come down to being *turned away by an attitude of indifference on the part of a company employee* (Journal of Marketing). A great EB should create an environment where that never happens, and Ipsos has shown the strong linkage between customer advocacy and employee advocacy. Walk into an Apple store to see that at its best.

For More Information

To find out more about employer brand management or People in Business (PiB), go to www.people-in-business.com or www.employerbrand.com; or email Simon Barrow directly at simon@pib.co.uk .

chapter seven | **Managing Talent**

Dick Antoine
CHRO, Procter & Gamble (retired)

Procter & Gamble is a multinational consumer products company founded in 1837. Famous for its iconic brands—Tide, Pampers and Crest among them—P&G is ranked fifth on Fortune *magazine's 2011 list of the "World's Most Admired Companies." This is the seventh straight year the company has ranked in the top ten. Based in Cincinnati, the company employs 130,000 people and had revenues of more than $82 billion in FY 2011. Dick Antoine retired as P&G's Global Human Resource Officer in 2008.*

If you ask any of P&G's senior leadership team, "What are the company's most important assets?", Dick Antoine says the responses, to a person, will be "Our brands and our people." P&G has 23 brands that each sells more than $1 billion around the world every year, which is a pretty remarkable record. And people are the other most important asset. "You can't replace those brands and you can't replace the people. Everything else is secondary to those," said Dick. "Unless the senior leaders truly believe that people are one of our two or three most important assets, then it's hard to build a great reputation for talent and it's hard to build great talent."

P&G does have a well-earned reputation for growing talent. The company is ranked third, both globally and in North America, in *Fortune* magazine's 2011 list of "Top Companies for Leaders." Aon Hewitt, which conducted the research on behalf of *Fortune*, described the top companies as being "passionate and committed to leadership development. Their leadership programs are practical, relevant and aligned with business goals. Top companies have an intense focus on talent, and they are deliberate about hiring, coaching, developing and rewarding success. Finally, leadership development at these organizations is an embedded practice and mindset." Dick couldn't agree more.

An Effective Talent Management System

P&G is committed to growing leaders from within, accomplished through a comprehensive talent management system. Their system is an integrated series of processes covering all aspects, from attracting to hiring to retaining to developing, that fit together to make sure that the organization gets the talent it needs, with the right skills at the right time. "Talent management is incredibly important; done right, it's what gives you the talent for the very top of the company," said Dick.

Making it work depends on a simple, but critical factor. "What really makes talent management systems succeed is line ownership. HR is responsible for developing the systems and the approaches. But unless the line owns it, you've just got an underutilized and unvalued HR system. Unless the business managers own the system, it doesn't work. They have to be involved in the hiring process and make the decisions about who gets hired in their organization. They have to be doing performance reviews. They have to be doing talent reviews, where you look at your top talent and succession plans. They need to spend a significant amount of time on this," Dick explained. He shared two anecdotes that illustrate his points.

The first relates to a benchmarking visit. From time to time, Dick and his team hosted their counterparts from other top companies to share information about P&G's talent management system. "We had a *Fortune* 50 company visiting us, and we had spent about an hour going through our philosophy, approaches and systems. The visiting CHRO interrupted our presentation to ask, in an incredulous manner, 'How do you get the line people to do this?' At first I was at a loss for words. Then I finally looked at her and said, 'Because it's their job.' I don't know if that's always the case in other companies, but I would hope so. HR can develop the most sophisticated talent management system in the world, but it's never going to work if the line doesn't own it."

The second anecdote is about an interview a reporter from a business publication was conducting with A.G. Lafley when he was P&G's CEO. Talent management was the topic of the interview, so Dick was sitting in. As Dick relayed the story, "A.G. was talking about the congruence of talent management with the business strategy and how the line has to own it. The reporter asked A.G., 'So, how much time do you spend on all these talent management activities—talent reviews, assignment planning and succession planning?' In other words, everything that we would say is part of the talent management system. A.G. paused for a moment; he was obviously thinking about it. And I'm thinking to myself, I have no idea what the answer is. Then A.G. said, '40 percent.' You could tell from the reporter's body language that he found it hard to believe that the CEO would be spending that much time on it.

"So I actually had his assistant take the last six months of A.G.'s calendar and highlight all the elements that were part of the talent management system to get a real calculation of his time. And it came out at 36 percent, which I figured was close enough to 40 percent to be reasonable. The CEO's spending that kind of time on people, on talent, backs up the assertion that people are truly one of our two most important assets."

Dick went on to explain that most P&G leaders probably spend 20 percent to 25 percent of their time on talent. "The majority of our leaders are developed and promoted from within. They've grown up with that system, and they've benefitted from it," said Dick. "They know they have an obligation to continue that system for the people who work for them."

In addition to line ownership, Dick outlined additional requirements for a successful talent management system. "People must have the opportunity to progress based on merit, rather than who you know or maybe even your style. We used objective scorecards to be clear on who was delivering the best results and who was falling short."

And the company has to provide training and development opportunities for people. Like the majority of HR leaders, Dick understands that the most effective development takes place on the job, not in a classroom (see pie chart, page 65). "We spent a lot of time figuring out the best match of a person with an assignment that will fulfill his or her development needs," said Dick. Often those assignments were what Dick's successor, Moheet Nagrath, calls "crucible roles": the really tough, demanding roles that stretch your best talent and gauge how they react. These include business turnarounds, acquisitions, new country entries and new category startups.

How Talent Develops

10%

10%

80%

- On-the-job experience, "crucible" roles
- Coaching from manager, mentor
- Formal training programs, classroom and online

Defining Talent

There are lots of definitions of talent, some more useful than others. Dick provided a definition that worked for him, in terms of the key characteristics that differentiate talented people.

First, they're bright. "In any organization, hire the smartest people you can find," advised Dick. "That doesn't necessarily mean GPA. But it does mean people who are thoughtful and knowledgeable about a broad range of topics. We looked for people who had some breadth in addition to just raw candle power."

Second, talented people are hard working. "In most successful companies you do work hard," Dick said. "We expected people to have that work ethic; it was part of the deal. Work hard and work effectively, and you'll be rewarded."

Third is the right skills. Talented people have the right skills and knowledge to do the job.

Fourth, those skills have to be applied to the business needs. As Dick wryly observed, "If you've got great talent working on something that the organization doesn't care about, you're running a hobby as opposed to a business."

Partner with people who are really good at creative work to help you with the messages.

Finally, true talent delivers outstanding results. "Talented people don't just mill around and say at the end of the quarter, 'Well, we were decent. We didn't cause any harm.' That's not what you're looking for from real talent," said Dick. "And I mean 'delivering outstanding results' in the broadest sense. It's not just about delivering profit or financial results. It's producing outstanding results in your area of expertise—IT, Marketing or HR. We measured both business *and* organization results. For the latter we tracked turnover, employee survey results, diversity and top talent development."

Partnering with PR

Marketing at P&G is solely focused on the marketplace and the company's products. The Public Relations (PR) staff is responsible for presenting the company with its best foot forward not just externally, but internally with employees as well. So when it came to building an employer brand, Dick and his team partnered with PR. "They're good at developing messages, and we in HR aren't. So you partner with the people who are really good at this kind of creative work to help you with the messages."

Those messages are all about P&G's employer brand, which has two major audiences. "You want the people internally to be proud of the organization, to go the extra mile, to be dedicated and passionate toward their company. And you want people externally to want to work for your company. That's what an employment brand is all about. Fortunately, P&G has a pretty good employer brand. Not exaggerating, I think it's one of the best in the world."

P&G's employer brand is clearly working for the external audience. Each year the company brings in about 5,000 new hires around the globe. To fill those positions, P&G gets half a million applications, so the company can be very selective in its hiring decisions. It's the great brand reputation that makes a lot of people around the world want to work for the company.

The company's reputation on the outside must match the employees' experience on the inside. For Dick, that's "part and parcel" of talent retention. "You've got to treat people fairly in terms of compensation, benefits, performance and career opportunities.

You also have to have a strong sense of purpose." Like Libby Sartain (see page 38), Dick pointed out that new college hires today are much more interested in the purpose of the organization and what it says about them and their need to be part of something important. "P&G's purpose is 'to improve the lives of the world's consumers, now and for generations to come.' That resonates with a number of people," Dick said.

Retaining Talent

A question we hadn't planned to ask Dick, but one that he wanted to answer, was why people, especially talented people, leave an organization. "HR routinely did exit interviews with people who left, and we got a set of answers that I would argue are the politically correct answers. Those answers are also true in some cases. But when we hired an independent company to ask the same question, when the responses were anonymous, we got a different set of answers. It was the same two answers almost every time. They left either because of their manager or insufficient career opportunities. That's why we spent a lot of time on training and development to make sure that people have managers who can lead and assignments that can challenge them."

The reasons people give for leaving an organization ...	
In exit interviews on their last day.	**To an independent—and anonymous—surveyor six months later.**
• I'm leaving because of a location problem. • I've got a family / spouse issue. • They just waved so much money at me I couldn't resist.	• My manager was a jerk. • They weren't offering me the opportunity to move up at the pace I felt was appropriate.

Making a Difference

Dick retired from HR, but that's not how he started out. "My whole career was in supply chain, mostly in the manufacturing part. When the CEO offered me the Global HR job, my first reaction was to turn around to see who he was talking to. When it became obvious that he meant me, I asked him why. He said that I had credibility with the line, that line leaders would like to see me in the role," Dick recounted. (See sidebar on page 70 for Dick's checklist for successful HR organizations.)

"I accepted the job, somewhat reluctantly. But after a couple of years, I totally changed my mind. I should have asked for this sooner, because you *can* make such a difference in the company from the CHRO role."

Dick Antoine's Checklist for Successful HR Organizations

HR plans and processes that align with business goals and strategies.

HR doesn't set strategy; it provides help and support to achieve the business goals and strategies. For example, if the company is expanding into a new geography or a different business line, HR has to identify the required skills and source the people to deliver that strategy.

Credibility with the line.

HR people have to understand the business so they can partner with line managers to understand their problems and find solutions. The line has little patience with "HR speak" or "You can't do that" police.

Technical competence in Human Resources.

HR people have to understand the laws and rules on benefits and executive compensation, for example, because they're responsible for compliance.

Both a service and cost control mentality.

All too often HR winds up in one camp or the other, when it's really a both/and situation. HR must balance the need to provide essential and valued services to employees with the requirement to manage the cost.

Ask the Partners

Q: HR is one of the most difficult roles within any company, and it's critical to the company's success. We make a huge difference, but it's not an obvious difference. As a career, HR just isn't sexy. Given that, how do we attract top talent into the HR profession? I think part of the challenge is that HR people need to have high personal self-confidence and relatively low ego. It's the business leader who gets the credit if things go well (as well as the blame if they don't). This "unpublicized excellence" is part of the dilemma.

A: We do it the old-fashioned way—one at a time, building critical mass as well as proof sources as we go. Your own experience at P&G provides perhaps the best approach. It's also how Anne Mulcahy got the top HR job at Xerox, several years before becoming CEO. Look for and court raw talent, individuals who display the essential characteristics you've identified, who have good track records somewhere else—in another discipline or even general management. Explain and demonstrate the opportunity and impact HR can have when we have the right people doing the right work. Promote and market your success stories, then coach and mentor the best talent who will grow and thrive in HR.

chapter eight | **Taking an Innovative Approach to Talent**

Dimitra Manis
SVP, Global Head of People, Thomson Reuters

Thomson Reuters is the world's leading provider of intelligent information for businesses and professionals. Using industry expertise and innovative technology, the company delivers critical information to decision-makers in the financial, legal, tax and accounting, healthcare and science, and media markets. Headquartered in New York, Thomson Reuters employs more than 55,000 people in over 100 countries. Dimitra Manis joined Thomson Reuters three years ago and was appointed to her current position in February 2012. Before Thomson Reuters, she held several international assignments and worked with the AXA Group and Nike. Dimitra began her career with Banking and Finance in her native Australia.

Dimitra Manis is bullish on talent. Building on her global experience in HR and applying some out-of-the-box thinking, she's developed an innovative approach to recruiting and developing the talent Thomson Reuters needs to succeed. For starters, Dimitra says talent is everyone's job. "It shouldn't be an issue for a talent function or HR; everybody's accountable." Every leader, Dimitra says, has a role to play in identifying and developing talent for the future.

Creating a Talent Mindset

"The talent mindset itself is one of our big key drivers. We've taken an organizational design (OD) approach to talent where we have the liberty to say, 'Everybody understands why talent's important, but why is it that we struggle to flow talent across our businesses and why is it that we ultimately don't like sharing our good talent with other people?' Every leader, every person needs to build talent. They need to make sure they nurture the talent that's required for the business and that we continually share this talent, allowing it to flow where it's needed the most."

All HR leaders have worked with managers who hang on to their best performers, in many cases well past the optimum time to move that individual to another position or function. The long-term benefit of developing talent is traded off for the short-term advantage of the manager's team performance. "That's why our talent mindset intervention is such a critical one," Dimitra explained. "Because it's all about helping people shift their mindsets, so that they can all contribute to the success of the whole company and think of talent as a whole, not just for themselves. Leaders need to display more selfless behavior when it comes to sharing talent. So the talent mindset is all about helping the organization—leaders and people—shift their head space. It's absolutely critical that we share the talent and set our talent free in the right areas, truly unleashing their potential."

Dimitra recognizes that talent is a perishable commodity. With a combination of communication and cajoling, she and her team developed an intervention that helps shift managers' mindsets so that they can go from hoarding talent to sharing it. Here's how Dimitra describes the ultimate outcome they're working toward. "When I ask a manager: 'Who's your best talent? And what are you doing with them?' The answer we are aiming for is, 'I'm moving them, stretching them and growing them because I want to develop them to the best of the organization.' Talent is high on everyone's agenda and critical for the business."

Segmentation Strategy

Thomson Reuters operates in several diverse market segments: financial, healthcare, legal, media, science and tax & accounting. Dimitra Manis has taken a similar approach to talent. "We have a segmentation strategy to talent. It's segmented, just as we do with our customers. We know which of our customers produce most of our revenue and future growth opportunities, and which customers need much more attention than others. And we've done the same with our talent. We've grouped our talent in five key segments and we focus on each segment differently. There are very different factors going on within each of those segments."

For example, retention is an issue with only one of the segments. "We retain talent extremely well," said Dimitra. "We deal with intelligent information, and we've got really smart people. The type of work we do really matters; we have meaning in our jobs. And that makes people want to stay. But we're losing more than our fair share in one segment, and we're actively addressing it."

The talent segments are different from the market segments. "They basically line up with our capabilities and the requirements for the business. So we've taken our business strategy and worked out which capabilities we need to focus on and which we might need less of. Each one of our segments is different. One of them, for example, is our global segment. Some people might automatically think that's our global talent. But actually, it's our local talent in those strategic global markets that we need to be in, that are critical to the success. No one has segmented talent and focused on it the way we have. We've taken a customer segmentation approach and brought that methodology to implement talent segmentation."

Collaborating Internally and Reaching out Externally

Like many of the HR leaders interviewed for this book, Dimitra works with her Strategy and Marketing colleagues, as well as business leaders and Operations people who work directly with customers. But Dimitra feels strongly that internal collaboration is just part of the story. "HR always focuses on the internal customer," she explained. "We actually forget that ultimately we're here for the end user, the end customer. And what we need to do is make sure that whatever we do with our employees, whatever we do to develop them or retain them or recruit them is all about achieving the end-customer goal.

"Getting people to understand that the customer experience is fundamentally part of the bigger agenda is one of the objectives that we have. We need to think about 'What do *we* need to do to help our employees deliver the optimum customer experience?' And that's what's key."

Dimitra's convictions drive her behavior. "I don't limit myself to just the Marketing and internal folks; I actually spend time with the customer," said Dimitra. Thomson Reuters sponsors periodic client conferences that provide a natural avenue for Dimitra to meet with clients. But she also reaches out to customers in less formal ways, meeting with them over coffee or lunch. [Authors' note: In most organizations, coordinating customer visits through the Sales organization would be the best approach.]

Consciously thinking about the end customer—I don't think we do that enough in HR.

"So I'm spending more and more time with our customers myself, meeting with them, talking with them, listening to them. Going to our client conferences and listening to what their concerns are and what their issues are. Getting to know our customers and what their requirements are. That helps me understand how to influence the direction of what our employees need, and how to define the type of talent we need."

For too long, Dimitra says, HR has done a poor job of having a direct interface with the end customer. "We need to make sure that whatever we do with our employees, whatever we do to develop them or retain them or recruit them is all about achieving the end-customer goal. People always talk about the importance of customers. But how many people actually spend time with the customer? How many people are really thinking about changing the profile of employees so that we can truly service our customers more effectively? Consciously thinking about the end customer—I don't think we do that enough in HR."

Ask the Partners

Q: I'd be interested in one thing that sticks out as being fundamentally fresh and innovative. I'd like to learn about one new thing that someone else in HR is doing that's really leading edge and real, true thought leadership in this field.

A: For thought leadership, it's hard to beat Jeff Joerres' Human Age positioning, a view that prompts reorienting business thinking and processes through a human lens. We also think that the overall premise of our book is new and innovative: looking at how some leading-edge companies are striving to make their brands live through their employees. Our contributors advise treating employees at least as well as customers, even making them your No. 1 priority to achieve inside-out branding, employee loyalty and improved business performance.

Another proof source on the last concept is Vineet Nayar's 2010 book, *Employees First, Customers Second: Turning Conventional Management Upside Down*, which *Fortune* magazine called "the world's most modern management idea." Nayar is CEO of HCL Technologies, a leading global IT services company. Under Nayar's leadership, the company inverted the pyramid, to create transparency and accountability and to encourage a value-driven culture. For example, 360-degree feedback on 1,500 managers is posted online for all employees to see—a practice that started with Nayar posting his own feedback. The results: Attrition is down, revenue per employee and customer satisfaction are up. Employees' effectiveness has improved and they now have a passion for their work.

chapter nine | **Looking at Talent from the Startup Perspective**

Marcel Legrand
Entrepreneur and Co-founding Member, Monster Worldwide

Marcel Legrand served as SVP of Strategy and Corporate Development and was one of the first employees at Monster.com, which launched in 1994; today it is one of the world's largest employment Web sites. Earlier in his tenure he served as SVP of Corporate Development at Monster.com, and SVP of Product at the parent company, Monster Worldwide, through 2006. Until 2010, Marcel was a partner at Blackfin Capital LLC, a private equity firm that invested in companies within the technology and healthcare services sector. Currently, he is co-founder of a new big data firm. He also serves as a board member and consultant for various startup investments funded by Tiger Global, Warburg Pincus and General Atlantic.

Marcel Legrand's experience with startups has provided him with a unique perspective on talent and the roles of HR and Marketing. The needs of a startup with five or ten pioneers are very different from those of an established company with hundreds or thousands of employees.

Talent

When he's looking for people to join his startup companies, Marcel has some very specific requirements. "I've been well-served by looking for characteristics that are beyond the individuals' past experience and more about their emotional intelligence (see definition below) and some of their behavioral habits to make sure they're a good cultural fit," Marcel said. "I'm looking for more than just book smarts. If we're trying to sell a new social networking tool to a media company, for example, they have to be a lot more imaginative and resourceful. They have to really understand the customer and be ready to pivot very quickly. In a new market, we're creating new behavior, and with that comes the need to adapt."

Emotional intelligence is the ability to identify, use, understand and manage emotions in positive and constructive ways. It's about recognizing one's own emotional state and the emotional states of others. Emotional intelligence is also about engaging with others in ways that draw people to you.

from El Skills Group

Flexibility is also important. Marcel looks for individuals who can work long, hard hours. "Pay" is usually more along the lines of the potential for future wealth through options than in salary here and now. Marcel acknowledged that this profile lends itself to a hungrier workforce that's willing to accept a work-life balance that favors the startup, as well as older, experienced and established talent willing to trade up for higher-risk wealth creation.

Startups sometimes make use of a hiring strategy that's virtually unheard of in more established companies. "I've had some success with what's been coined 'try before you buy.' The candidate and I look at each other through the interview process, and if we think there's a mutual fit, we agree that we're going to give it six months. Reciprocal fitness can't be measured in an interview—it must be battle tested in the real world. After 180 days, if we're not a good fit for each other, all bets are off. There are no expectations that things are guaranteed. And I think it's very, very important to set up those expectations. It allows you to see people in action and not necessarily feel compelled to keep them if they're not really fitting the culture, or vice versa if the company does not meet the candidate's expectations."

Marcel's reasoning is straightforward: "At a startup stage, you really can't compromise with talent. I think you have a lot more latitude in an established company. When you have 5,000 people, then two or three, or 10 or even 100 mismatched employees won't kill the company. But when your team is 10 or 11 people iterating on a product, with high stakes and little forgiveness, there's no margin for error. Every one of them is absolutely critical—their output, their approach and their attitude. And if those things aren't working like a well-oiled machine, you have to make decisions and changes very quickly."

Marketing First, Then HR

Marcel believes that Marketing and HR should be aligned on how a company brands itself and communicates to constituents. But in a startup, Marketing comes first. "In a consumer-driven company, Marketing tends to come up much sooner because it has more immediate revenue impacts. It's probably one of the first four key hires," explained Marcel. "I've never had or heard of an HR person in an organization for the first two years of a startup. Initially, the administrative things, like payroll and compliance, can be outsourced at very little cost. Additionally, and more important, the HR role around talent is something I expect from the first 20 founders coming in. Everybody has to own the decisions about who comes on board—that's what builds a culture."

As the company matures, Marcel sees HR coming into its own. "I think that HR has a critical function at a tipping point, which depends on the size and maturity of your business. You really do need to bring in a professional who can run point around compliance and look at talent and performance measurements in a way that you're not able to on a day-to-day basis. Getting the most out of HR is really about pragmatic timing."

Along with talent, part of the HR role involves collaborating with Marketing. "I believe that the two functions should be well-aligned relative to how the firm develops their brand and communications strategy, and who's saying what. If you really do believe that the confluence of Marketing and HR comes together in employer branding, and both people agree with it, it's powerful and can increase value exponentially."

But Marcel acknowledged that there can be friction. "If the HR staff doesn't understand marketing, and the marketer is questioning HR's influence and value in the process, you have a problem. The fact that Marketing gets in earlier doesn't necessarily give them the upper hand in the collaboration," said Marcel. "It really does come down to the executives setting the tone early on, and explaining to the head of Marketing, 'Employer branding is one of the areas you need to influence, but as a team.'"

If Marketing and HR come together in employer branding, it's powerful.

The Impact of Social Media

Marcel observed that "Twenty years ago, it was very clear that you _managed_ your reputation, both from an advertising and branding perspective. In today's environment, you _participate_ in your reputation. Social media platforms have created situations such that a lot of people who may be disenfranchised with you now have a platform to share that with others." He gave the example of a Starbucks barista who's had a bad day. She isn't afraid of tweeting to the world about what an awful place Starbucks can be to work. "It's now incumbent on the company to help manage its reputation, to go back and find the influencers and try to change the sentiment, through its actions and online. They can try to reach out to employees and say, 'You weren't willing to tell you boss why you have bad days. But tell us, with some anonymity.' In the past you spent ad dollars telling the world what you were about; now you also have to spend time and money changing hearts and minds online because others have a say in your brand reputation, both employer and commercial."

That hypothetical situation matches one from Marcel's own experience. "It was a venture capitalist-backed startup that I had also invested in personally. We found out that employees were actually tweeting about their day and some of their managers, and about what they did or didn't believe about the business. The investors found out and said, 'Have you seen this? You have to take control.' The fact is you can't control the people. But you do have to start controlling the reputation of the business. We're definitely heading into that direction."

Marcel pointed out that this is another area where HR could use a lot of Marketing support. "Marketing is so well-attuned to online advertising and sentiment monitoring in a way that HR is not. HR is responsible for setting policies around employees' use of social media, but Marketing is much better prepared on the communications side of that space. So it's a new competency where they both would be well-served by combining their forces," said Marcel.

A Great Place to Work

To Marcel, "The truest measure of a great workplace is going to be a reflection of three things:

- What you do,

- How you're allowed to do it, and

- With and for whom you do it."

The last is by far the most important. Like Dick Antoine (see page 61), Marcel is keenly aware of a manager's role in retaining talent. "Anybody who spends more than two to three years in an employment environment realizes that people don't work for companies; they work for people," he said. "One bad manager can completely dilute any goodwill an employer provides for its workforce. If turnover is an issue, you need to start by examining their managers. When employees leave, it's most often a result of who they work for—people leave people, not companies. Exit interviews administered at most companies are so often unable to identify this issue; so the real motives are never captured."

Marcel has a solution that's worked for him. "In the companies where I've had a leadership position, I make sure, formally and informally, that each manager is measured with anonymity by their direct reports. Employees' forthright feedback on their bosses is a canary in the coal mine for me. If you fail to do that and only administer reviews of subordinates by their bosses, it's like putting a band-aid on an aneurysm. You may have great results, but those employees will turn over in the next year and go to the competition.

"The emphasis here is _how_ a manager achieves results, not just their outcomes. This is where I think HR's competency plays its strengths. They're looking at some of the softer skills. The marketer says, 'What are the numbers? The numbers say the manager's great.' But an HR person might take a deep dive and do a couple interviews with some people and say, 'The numbers may look good, but how the manager achieved them—that's questionable.'"

85

Valuing People

As we wrapped up, Marcel touched on a issue that he's been concerned about for a number of years. "In the discussions I've had with Will about Marketing and HR, one of the disconnects is that Marketing has the science of sales. It's heavily focused on measurement—numbers, movement, qualifying and quantifying things. Traditionally, HR has taken a bit of a softer approach. They're now moving to some of the metrics that are expected of them, things like cost per hire, success per path of hire, average revenue per employee and productivity metrics."

But there is still what Marcel called the massive conundrum of how you value employees. "When I make a hire, it immediately becomes a liability on my financial statements. Payroll, one of the largest categories in anybody's P&L, is looked at as an expense. But in a knowledge environment, the people who walk in and out each day are the true assets. It's not the number of servers or retail locations that create value. In the end, Caribou Coffee and Seattle's Best and Starbucks serve the same coffee. It's all in the personal delivery and the environment that the employees build—this is where unique propositions lie. We talk a lot about how that's the differentiator, but nobody is able to put their arms around it yet. Contribution margin per employee; getting to that is extremely difficult for anybody and will be one of the great financial and human capital measures of our time."

Ask the Partners

Q: The pervasiveness of contract, freelance and outsourced hires by an employer is making it more difficult to impact your employer brand. Let's say that today, 20 percent of most companies' hires or workforce are part-time/contract employees. A large part of your army is marching to a different drum. They really do have a different message and a different perspective on supporting your employer brand. This is a trend that we expect to continue. And if that happens, how can you expect these employees to be brand ambassadors for your firm, with your message and your passions?

A: A company's goal is to provide strategic relevance to its customers in the form of goods, technology and services. If all employees—part-time, full-time, seasonal, freelance—are aligned properly to the company's goals, they should be able to be of strategic relevance to customers.

You can create alignment by connecting strategic relevance to the company's brand and communicating that as part of onboarding for all types of hires. Then reinforce through ongoing communications on business performance, customer satisfaction and "wins" in the marketplace.

chapter ten | **Partnering with Marketing**

Mary Eckenrod
Vice President, Global Talent Solutions, Research In Motion

*Research In Motion (RIM), the company behind BlackBerry®
smartphones, is based in Ontario, Canada. Mary Eckenrod leads
RIM's Global Talent Solutions. Prior to RIM, Mary led global talent
management for several other high-tech companies including Cisco
Systems, Rockwell and Lenovo, with extensive experience in
Europe and Asia. Mary serves on the Advisory Board, Center for
Effective Organizations (USC), and was formerly Board Chair of the
Human Resources Planning Society.*

When RIM's Talent Solutions team embarked on an internal
employer branding initiative, the Marketing team was the first to be
consulted. "You can't have one message on the outside that your
employees see and hear while a different message exists internally.
The story you tell has to be consistent, whether the audience is
prospective customers, current employees or future talent."

Integrating and Reinforcing the Messages

"We invited the branding people to work with us, to start to identify
what was important in messaging. What were we saying to our
customers that could help us drive the behaviors and values needed
to deliver on our customer promise? What expectations do we have
of our people? We discovered that we had some of that messaging
in place. It just wasn't packaged in a way that we could look at it and

say, 'These are the values and expectations of our people. This is what we embody every day in what we do. This is what and how we deliver on customer expectations.'

"It wasn't a big aha moment or anything like that. It was recognizing 'We need to get the right people in the room, and work together on this. Let's make sure that we're aligned with our messages.' We can partner with Marketing by putting this into the context of what we're training employees on and how we're assessing our people. We can tell people, 'These are our shared values. These are the behaviors that enable us to deliver what our customers want. These things are important for a successful career at RIM.'"

The result has been win-win. "It's been a true partnership, and we've benefitted from each other. As Marketing has shared with us, 'Here's how we're going at the new branding campaigns,' we recognize that it's not all that different from what we try to do internally. So we connect and integrate it. There are huge synergies between what we do in our two organizations."

To check that they're on the right track, the Talent Solutions team conducted employee focus groups. The feedback was generally positive, but employees identified a gap. "They told us that we weren't making the best use of our own employees to be BlackBerry brand ambassadors."

"Talk BlackBerry" was the result. It's a series of short, 10-15 minute e-learning modules, one for each new product, available on *Learn@RIM*, the company's learning portal. Mary explained, "We highlight new product features for employees, why they're important, and what's competitive. This knowledge helps our people become brand and product ambassadors. The Marketing people assist and provide sponsorship. They help us understand the core messages and present them in a way that's consistent with what we're saying on the Sales side. These modules have been a hit with employees."

Reflecting on why the partnership with Marketing people has been so successful, Mary focused on their skill set. "The best Marketing people are very astute psychologists. They understand what motivates people, how people think, why people buy a device. Why wouldn't you want to integrate that with your HR practices? It's a great partnership. There's a huge opportunity to share what we know about people and how to do a better job of engaging them, internally and externally. The Marketing lessons on how to encourage new customers and keep your existing customers are exactly what we ought to understand and use internally. We consistently need to engage with our employees."

Mary's advice to HR leaders is simple and direct. "HR should focus on how to integrate messages, re-engaging and reinforcing it with employees. Integration and reinforcement are critical."

Attracting and Keeping Talent

With Global Talent Solutions in her title, it seemed natural to ask Mary to define talent and share what it takes to attract and retain talent in the high-tech world. "When I identify somebody as a key talent in the organization, I think about someone who can take on broader responsibilities, and has the ability to move within the organization and make a difference. He or she can go across boundaries; they can move into different roles. They can influence and change people's thinking. They're future leaders—people leaders and technology leaders."

RIM is smart enough to offer dual career tracks. "Sometimes you find that your most innovative people don't do well managing a team. They prefer to work with the product, solving technical challenges. Then you have individuals who are great people leaders. You need both, and the better technology companies don't force people who are really good at technology to manage a team of people."

Working with Marketing, we've helped our people become brand ambassadors.

As for what talented people are looking for in a potential employer, Mary had a list of a half dozen characteristics that, in her experience, particularly appeal to Gen Y talent. This list is in addition to what Mary calls "table stakes": reasonably competitive pay and benefits, along with factors like a safe workplace. "You've got to have those things; they're the basics people expect. But they won't inspire people to join and stay with an employer."

Fun. The first item on Mary's list was fun. "It means different things to different people, and it's generational to a degree. To many twenty-somethings, 'fun' means the ability to work in teams, to collaborate, to do 'cool stuff.' To a scientist, it could be 'let me tinker and build the things that could be the next generation of technology.'"

The opportunity to contribute. "Talented people want to have an impact and make a difference. They want to have a voice in making decisions about what they do and how they do it."

Growth. "People like to be associated with companies that are growing. Beyond revenue growth and market share, I tend to equate growth with going into parts of the world where you haven't had much experience, to be part of those emerging markets. Growth has to be a joint proposition, meeting the needs of the company and individual."

Open communications. "This loops back to the need for consistent internal and external messages. The reputation on the outside has to match the experience on the inside. Your people need to understand your general direction as an organization."

Minimal bureaucracy. "Tech people have a different view of what makes a company a great place to work. It's critical to demonstrate that bureaucracy doesn't get in the way of being fast and responsive to competitive challenges."

Innovation and risk taking. Mary used her own industry as an example. "Six years ago there were mostly mobile phones with a few smart devices. Look at the industry today; tablets, smartphones and a growing set of competitors, many based in Asia. You have to be able to take some risks; it's all part of the innovation formula. If you have a reputation as a company that's willing to take risks and innovate, it attracts people. It's a fun place to work."

As for retention, Mary eloquently summed up why people want to stay and build their careers with an employer: "It allows me the opportunity to become someone I couldn't be anywhere else. There's something unique about what this organization offers that I'm engaged and inspired to stay. I know I couldn't replicate that feeling, those career opportunities, the networking with my team or the quality of leadership. I couldn't find that somewhere else."

That's the way we should all feel.

Ask the Partners

Q: Many companies are challenged to fully engage their people. How do we take what we know about Marketing, engaging customers and get our leaders to understand that they have to market their organization to their people? That every day it's important to realize that their employees, the inner workings of what makes their company unique and their talent are just as important as their customers. How can we help them take the external messaging and bring it inside? There are some very enlightened leaders. But there's just as many out there who don't get it.

A: Take the initiative; attack the problem as you would a major Marketing campaign. Here are some ideas we think worth exploring: Draft communications for your CEO to recognize and thank employees for their accomplishments. Work with your internal communications group to make people/talent a standard part of all earnings announcements. Partner with Marketing to use social media to solicit comments from key customers about employees who have gone above and beyond. Use your company's intranet to ask managers to share case studies of employees and teams who have achieved extraordinary results—and show how these link to the company's goals. The very actions you take to solicit input from customers and managers are likely to create some buzz—and that's a good thing.

People are a major asset class—along with brand, products, infrastructure and cash. We would never expect to have a senior leadership team or board meeting that didn't include a discussion of the company's finances. The same should hold true for talent, so that leaders recognize the role they must play in nurturing and supporting the human assets of the enterprise. But it's up to HR to make sure that leaders have something important to say and a blueprint for action—and ultimately the future talent to lead and inspire organization.

chapter eleven | **Thinking Outside the Box**

Telvin Jeffries
Executive VP, Human Resources, Kohl's Corporation

Wisconsin-based Kohl's is one of the country's largest retailers. With a presence in every state but Hawaii, the company operates more than 1,100 stores and has almost 140,000 associates. Kohl's focuses on style, quality and value, offering customers a mix of national and private-label brands. For FY 2011, Kohl's reported revenues of $18.8 billion. Kohl's has been recognized for its social awareness program "Kohl's Cares," which supports kids' health and education initiatives and women's health. The company has also received several awards for green programs in support of its mission to be a leading environmentally responsible retailer. Telvin Jeffries joined Kohl's in 1993; he was named to the top HR position in 2003.

Telvin Jeffries spends a lot of time thinking. He thinks about how to bring metrics and discipline to the HR function. He thinks outside the box when it comes to sourcing people for his senior team. He thinks about how to keep his large HR organization connected and in the loop. Most recently, he's focused on trying to figure out the next big thing for the HR profession.

A Collaborative Environment

Telvin described effective work environments as highly collaborative. "We as HR leaders need to make sure that all our key stakeholders are aware of what we're doing. They can give us feedback about how we should make adjustments so that we don't derail each other's projects. But it doesn't mean the projects stop. It means we have to buy in and be supportive. We don't always have to agree, but we do have to be informed. By informed, I don't mean they find out through a mass email or posting on a company Web site. I mean they find out personally from me. People will take affront if they're left out of the loop. I always make sure that new HR people know that."

That spirit of collaboration applies to HR and Marketing. "The head of Marketing and the head of HR should meet on a regular basis, for example, twice a month. They should talk to each other about a diverse array of topics that over time grows in scope. Marketing leads the brand message, and the CHRO's job is to understand the messaging, vision and goals. Then he or she should go back to his or her organization, make sure everything they do is aligned with that brand messaging, from the way people are hired, to the way they are trained and rewarded."

Telvin went on to provide an example. "One of our taglines at Kohl's is 'Expect great things.' When we developed that, our CMO and I spent a lot of time talking about what that means, and especially how it would affect our associates. There was a clear partnership about the messaging and the tools that we would use to roll out the new tagline to our associates."

Telvin cited another example of this partnership, pointing to a tool his training team developed last year to support a customer service initiative. "HR created a game that we gave to every store manager. It was a learning map, based on our store. It mapped all the touchpoints that send customers messages that align with our customer service initiative. With the help of that tool, every store manager sat down and talked with all 150 to 200 of their associates, in groups of five or six."

As part of their regular meetings, Telvin shared plans for the program with the Chief Marketing Officer. He explained, "Marketing was brought into the program to help us get the concept right. Human Resources knows how to get the content right and how adults learn, but Marketing helped us present the program with power and impact to our associates. We also didn't want to create anything that conflicted with the brand. We've learned that things as simple as color, style, even the syntax that's used, can actually send the wrong message." This year, Telvin and his team are building on their success by taking Kohl's customer service initiative to the next level. "It was probably the first time that every store manager had these types of resources to talk to all their 200 associates with a unified message. We want to facilitate more of that."

Another area of collaboration—in this case, a three-way collaboration—is the annual objective-setting process. "It's all about creating very clear objectives that everyone can buy into. Through the partnership of senior leadership, Marketing and HR, the group should work very hard to figure out:

- What are our business objectives going to be for the year?

- How can we make those objectives absolutely clear?

- How can we make sure everybody can play a part in those objectives?

Companies should hold their leaders responsible for breaking those objectives down into pieces that are, as I like to say, 'chewable.' HR plays an active role in breaking the objectives down into actionable goals and applicable messages for all our associates."

From the context, it was clear that, to Telvin, "chewable" means not only digestible, but also palatable. "It has to be," Telvin said, "because there's a value proposition. When you think about execution, it's not an issue of intellectual capacity alone; it's an issue of value to the employee. Each person has his or her own value proposition, but it comes down to recognition and awards. So if you come up with very grandiose objectives that don't match up with the value proposition for that person, our ability to execute is minimized. From the associates' point of view, the question is, 'Are you breaking things down so that I can clearly see why I should do this?' At the end of the day, they all want to contribute, they just want to know how and why."

Two-way Communications

Telvin understands the value of two-way communications with people in his HR organization. It's a large group—about 490 in all—and it takes a lot of work to keep everyone connected. Telvin focuses on three communication processes.

Manager Roundtables

Telvin holds several roundtables throughout the year with the 100 or so senior managers and managers in HR. In general, these participants are four levels below EVP. "I usually have two or three topics that I want to be sure they're clear about. I share things that we're working on and hope we can bring to fruition, giving them advance notice. And then it's open door to them. The feedback has been overwhelmingly positive. I share information that they might not otherwise hear, and they share insights with me that I might not otherwise hear. They also get to ask questions and get answers that are real. As you can tell, I generally don't hold back. The whole thing is genuine and authentic. I appreciate that and I think they do too."

Tea with Telvin

About once a month he hosts what he calls "Tea with Telvin," a more personal conversation with six individual contributors and nonexempt staff held in his office. Participants are selected on a rotation basis. As with the manager roundtables, Telvin shares upcoming projects, though in somewhat less detail. The point of these discussions is to invite the HR associates to ask questions of Telvin or bring up issues of concern to them. "They tell me things that happen within HR, and in the company, from a vantage point that, quite honestly, I'm sheltered from. It's a safe environment. Participants have learned, over the last three years, that I don't reveal sources. It's taken time for them to know that's how it works. At first they didn't say anything. Now they know I won't repeat it, but when necessary will act on it."

Online Chats

The third plank of Telvin's communications strategy is the biggest—
and the toughest: hosting a department-wide online chat session.
The size of the group is a complicating factor. "I usually ask four or
five questions to generate conversation. And they're talking to each
other; they're talking to me: 'What is training and development
working on that everybody else needs to know about? What's the
hottest thing you've heard about in recruiting recently?' So they'll all
type to each other, back and forth. The only problem with it," Telvin
said with a resigned chuckle, "is that I personally can't keep up with
the responses. It's 20 people shooting you comments, and they all
expect you to respond."

Telvin hasn't hosted an online chat for several months, but he
acknowledged that people keep asking for it. He likes the timeliness
and immediacy, but is looking for a more effective way to manage
the process for such a large group. Telvin's initiative has started a
trend. "I've shared it with other people in the company, and other
departments use it now. But they're smaller organizations. It works
great for a 30-40-person team."

Looking for Talent in All the Right Places

Telvin tries to build his HR leadership team in nontraditional ways by
looking for diversity of thought rather than rigid definitions of what
traditional roles would call for. A few examples include:

- The head of Leadership Development came from GE. Here's the
  challenge Telvin issued: "I said, 'Don't bring me everything that
  GE did and try to do it here. It won't work; it will die before it gets

started. But there are principles that you learned there that are true everywhere. Take those and "Kohl-ize" them, make them work in our environment.'"

- The head of Training and Development is an engineer who previously ran John Deere University.

- The executive responsible for HR services—compensation, benefits, learning, OD—was formerly an SVP of retail operations, responsible for Kohl's stores in half of the country. "We convinced her that her running HR support for the whole country would require the same skills she used in running retail for half the country. She's a great balance of operations and creativity, which is exactly what we need in that job."

- Telvin also has a direct report, an attorney who previously worked for an appellate judge, then spent a year working for Hewitt Associates as an executive compensation consultant, whom he uses to find solutions to a variety of complex issues.

In summary, Telvin looks for his HR people with diversity of thought. He likes people with backgrounds ranging from aerospace to consumer product goods to retail. He's looking for both analytical and creative people.

Having that combination is important in the retail world. Here's how Telvin explained his position. "Every company has people whose main role is to be creative. HR people have to go to those people with the creative mindset and say, 'I understand you're going to do a rollout of a new line. You tell me you're going to need X number of new people to do that. Now let's talk about what that will look like and the impact to the organization and our associates.'

"HR doesn't always fill this role, but over time it can develop templates and metrics that get to the best possible place. When that happens, business partners will seek out HR to help them with these issues and more. I've experienced this success firsthand."

The Next Big Thing

Telvin is looking ahead to the next big thing in HR (see his question, page 105). Right now he admits to not knowing exactly what it is, or even the best way to get to it. But he's got an intuitive feeling that it's not administrative efficiency. It's something much bigger, something revolutionary.

There was a clear partnership between HR and Marketing about the messaging and the tools.

Part of the answer may lie in a group called MiKE, which stands for, quite literally, "innovation in Milwaukee." (MKE is the airport code for Milwaukee.) Telvin is co-chair of the organization. "Our job is to make sure that we align business interests, higher education, technology and entrepreneurs together in our community. For example, we're connecting students to the companies. A lot of these people do not view a large, complex environment as their ideal place to work. Some of them feel most productive in smaller, open-concept environments. We're going to give them our business problems and we're going to let them hack away at ideas. They're going to create something that is going to change customer experience. To me, we have to get out of our box, get out of our offices, and connect to where stuff is happening."

Some Final Thoughts on the Role of HR

"I like to say that the CHRO should really be a leader or facilitator of the corporate ecosystem. Because we have a community that has outputs, and the outputs to me really are solutions to business problems or solutions that will help us be more competitive, or ideas that will clearly make us more competitive or solve problems or make us breakaway. There are the services we provide to keep our businesses going to meet the basic needs of our customers, our suppliers, and our vendors. But there's also the services that we provide to each other. That's what makes it an ecosystem.

"If I'm successful at execution, it's really because of the people I've surrounded myself with. They're wired around execution. What I can do for them—and by the way, it's not always easy—is to set the vision and remove the barriers. The words that I always use with HR people are, 'Our job is to help all the stakeholders achieve the outputs in the most effective and ethical way we can.' That's where HR comes in; we're the filter. And when I say 'ethically,' I use it in a very broad sense of the term."

Ask the Partners

Q: We're all doing a pretty good job in getting our arms around our ability to leverage technology and innovation when it comes to efficiency and administration. One of the questions I think we have to think about—and this is a new thing for me—is: What is the methodology that we should be using to apply innovation and technology in a way that makes HR better and breakaway in terms of our discipline, something that actually revolutionizes the way we do HR? You get to those things, I think, by deciding the methodology and how you will approach the particular tool. What are we missing? And who could we be mining from to help?

A: We're firm believers that to do things differently you must first see things differently. Helping people see the work of HR and Marketing in a new light was one of the motivators for producing this book. Your question about methodology seems to get at the "seeing differently" part of the equation.

We believe that contributor Jeff Joerres' thinking on The Human Age (see page 25) could provide a new lens through which to examine the work of HR. The Human Age implies fundamental changes in how people work, how they develop skills, how companies will source workers in the future, even the very definition of talent—all of which are within the purview of HR. You might consider pulling together a small team—Kohl's employees and some of the students you're working with at MiKE. Use the background on the Human Age as a springboard for a brainstorming session and see what develops.

chapter twelve | **Offering a Different Perspective**

Tom Maddison
VP, Human Resources, Xerox Corporation

Founded in 1906 as The Haloid Company, Xerox is a leader in document technology and services, providing printers, multifunction devices, production publishing systems and related software. With the February 2010 acquisition of Affiliated Computer Services, Xerox became the world's leading enterprise for business process and document management, offering global services from claims reimbursement and automated toll transactions to customer care centers and HR benefits management. The company has 140,000 employees in 160 countries. In 2011, Xerox had $22.6 billion in revenue. In February 2010, Tom succeeded Pat Nazemetz as Vice President of HR. He is responsible for human resource planning, sourcing, talent management, leadership development, pay, diversity and work environment.

Tom Maddison shares John Daniels' belief in the transformative power of organizations. "When we talk about differentiating one employer from another, it is absolutely not about a commercial relationship. It's about the transformative relationship, about transforming and evolving individuals. HR's role is to challenge the view that you should work here because we're going to pay you. The right answer is that working with us, you will become all you can become. We will facilitate and enable your development by providing appropriate challenges for you and your capability at every point."

That means creating an environment that enables people to perform and to be successful. It implies direction, clarity of objectives with the right level of precision, as well as feedback mechanisms that tell people how they're doing. For Tom, HR also has a role to play in helping the organization understand the value of people, not just the cost. "I believe the idea of increasing productivity by reducing the unit cost of labor is false," Tom said. "Real productivity comes from increasing the value people bring, not reducing the cost of people. Humans are generally very ineffective from a cost point of view, but highly effective from the value point of view. They make people feel cared for; they spot patterns that systems can't. HR has a role to play in helping the organization understand the value of people: why people are valuable, where they are most valuable and where that value may be declining."

Tom's convictions have led him to view terms like *employee value proposition* and *employer brand* somewhat skeptically. But he does see value in bringing clarity to the relationship between employer and employee, and to projecting the company to potential employees. Tom has given a great deal of thought to both employee value proposition and brand since Xerox's 2010 acquisition of Affiliated Computer Services (ACS), a move that increased the Xerox employee population by 250 percent, from 54,000 to 140,000. He offers a rather different and slightly provocative perspective.

Focusing on Win-Win

Tom doesn't believe that *employee value proposition* does a very good job of capturing the complex, multilayered relationship between employer and employee. What's worse, Tom said,

"Employee value proposition implies trade, and trade implies win-lose. Pay is win-lose. I give it to you. You have it; I have it no longer. That's win-lose. Your time. You dedicate your time to the company; you don't have it any more. And I don't believe the really valuable thing about working in an organization has very much to do with those things, other than as boundary conditions. You can't afford to work for nothing, because you need an income; that's a boundary condition. We're working with employee value proposition, using the framework that the Corporate Leadership Council (CLC) developed. What's important to me about the employee value proposition is focusing on the win-win components, like development." The table below lists Tom's win-win elements and his explanations.

Win-Win Elements of an Employee Value Proposition	
Development	"I spend $1,000 on your development. You've got $1,000 worth of development; I have an employee in the organization who's worth $2,000 more."
Meritocracy	"The best performers get the best opportunities. Great for you. And great for us because the best performers get developed."
Empowerment	"If we empower you to do the right things, you win because you build capability and create opportunity. And we win—the company, the customers and the shareholders."
Quality of Manager	"If we invest in quality of manager, the employee wins, the manager wins and the company wins."
Respect	"I think respect is an enormously powerful tool for leaders and managers of an enterprise. Respect can sit within the employee value proposition of any organization. And it costs you nothing."

Marketing and HR: Having and Being

A native Briton, Tom started his Xerox career in the UK. Before relocating to the United States in 2004, he managed both HR and Marketing, which were combined at the time. Based on that experience, Tom sees Marketing and HR as two disciplines that both draw on the fundamentals of human psychology and communications. But he also sees an essential difference.

"I think Marketing is trying to persuade somebody to consider and make a decision. And I think HR is doing some of that. But I also think one of the things we're communicating is meaning for our people, and we're trying to communicate with as much transparency as possible. HR is responsible for helping people understand meaning and purpose in the work they do. Erich Fromm wrote a great book called *To Have or To Be*. And I think this is the difference between HR and Marketing. Marketing's intention is all about *to have*; and HR's intention is all about *to be*. In the long term, it's about growing capability and developing that individual.

"If we talk about brand as an expression of value, commitment and promise, we start to line up some of the fundamentals back to humanity. There, both Marketing and HR draw from the same source, which is the source of purpose and meaning and work, a company's superordinate goal. Then I think you can say both of those disciplines are getting into values that people hold—whether those values are about excellence, creativity or service. I think where both HR and Marketing draw on a superordinate goal, something beyond the individual, and communicate that in the brand, then they're both trying to create meaning and purpose in human existence. So I think Marketing as a sales tool is different from Marketing as an alignment to values tool.

"Once you start talking about brand as it aligns to values and commitment, I think you can then say both HR and Marketing are trying to create an alignment to something bigger and more important than the individual, and that's a very healthy thing."

Brand and Values

Tom sees brand as the expression of a personality. "And with that," he explains, "comes an expectation of how someone behaves. It's a shorthand for a whole series of emotional and intellectual responses to something, and that creates a level of predictability. That's very powerful because predictability is incredibly important to people with regard to risk. You basically take some risk away with brand. When we say a company brand is recognized, I think we're saying we know them. We know this entity called Apple or IBM or Walmart. Marketers love that; they can work with it and project it."

But Tom has reservations about employer branding. "I think employees are so committed to an employer that a brand is actually a bit too thin. It needs to be more. It does need to be values and commitment. You want an employee to know a company in a much more intimate, more personal way than a brand suggests. And it's not about a single promise; it's about regular promises. It's not an abstract; it's about a very concrete series of events and actions that occur."

So what resonates with Tom? Values, as he intimated above. "I absolutely believe that employees need to be an expression of the company's values. Brand is a vehicle for expressing values. But before brand come values. So rather than saying employees are the expression of the brand, I prefer to say that employees are expressions of the values. And the brand is an expression of the values. They both draw from the same source, not one from the other, not one ahead of or behind the other."

When employees know a company intimately, when they are true expressions of its values, they become effective recruiters. "I'm keen on employee referrals as a means of hiring people because you want them to know the truth about you, warts and all. Attracting people to a business is easy. Attracting the *right* people is not so easy. You want people who say, 'Actually, the bad things about that company I don't mind too much. But the good things I really love. They don't pay as well, but you get great opportunities with regard to career.' Or conversely: 'You don't get great opportunities with regard to career, but they pay you really well.' You want people who fit; you want them to stay."

Aligning Xerox and ACS

On the surface, Xerox and ACS appear to have very different employee populations. Looking at the two organizations in commercial terms—pay and benefits—they initially appeared to be polar opposites. "But if you start thinking about the employee value proposition in the sense of meritocracy, opportunity to develop and empowerment, you can find an alignment across very different workforce segments," Tom said. "If you focus on the win-win elements, there really isn't a difference between a low-cost labor provider and a high-cost labor provider. For example, quality of manager is as important, if not more so, in a low-cost labor force. I think the things that are win-win are valuable across entities and enable you to create consistency in those aspects of your employee value proposition. So I think bringing the two organizations together became relatively simple, rather than the conundrum it first appeared to be."

HR is responsible for helping people understand meaning and purpose in the work they do.

Bringing the two organizations together also forced each to hold up a mirror to examine itself and look for differences and commonalities. "Xerox has a strong, global brand. ACS has limited brand recognition," said Tom. "What do they have in common? Innovation and service. I think both organizations have a long history of innovation. ACS from an entrepreneurial/innovative perspective, because of the way it grew. Xerox from a technical innovation perspective. But they're both innovative at their core of their belief set.

"Service is another core tenet. With its quality history, Xerox has built a commitment and dedication to the customer. Because our business model was very service oriented, in a technical service sense. And in the sense of helping the customer. ACS is very, very focused on service. Very responsive to the customer. I think those things are absolutely common. We can align around innovation and service at the very core."

The differences, especially brand, also played a role. "Xerox has a truly global brand; ACS didn't have a global footprint. Suddenly you can create huge value for that organization by leveraging Xerox's global brand and relationships. On the other hand, ACS brings an entrepreneurial spirit that large organizations often lose and gives Xerox the capability to do things it had brand permission to do. When you talk to people in ACS, they love the fact that Xerox has a brand, they love the value of that brand. You talk to people in Xerox, they're fascinated by ACS's entrepreneurial experience and attitude and approach. So in the end, the way to bring the two organizations together is see the commonalities and use the differences to create additional value that both sides perceive."

Adding Value (Literally) to Strategic Workforce Planning

For Tom, strategic workforce planning is about knowing your work. "The purpose of HR is producing a workforce. Our product is the right workforce to execute our strategy at the right time. Strategic workforce planning is a fundamentally different thing to headcount planning, cost planning. It's about aligning the value of employees with the value the company wants to bring to the marketplace."

Tom and his team built a toolkit to facilitate the right discussions with business leaders, focusing them on:

- What is it about your workforce that is valuable and important and will continue to be so?
- What is it about your workforce that is valuable and important today and may not continue to be so?
- What is it about your workforce that isn't important today but will be in the future?

At the end of his first year as VP, Tom met with every leader in the business and asked them very simple questions – not "How well is HR doing?" – but rather questions focused on the outcome:

- Do you have the workforce you need to execute the strategy?
- Do you have a pipeline of workforce that will help you execute it in the future?
- Is it productive?
- Is it cost effective?

If appropriate, Tom then followed up with second-level questions around effectiveness:

- Do you have the leadership you need?
- Do you have a workforce and organization design?
- Do you have the talent to populate that organization?
- And do you have the right work environment?

Ask the Partners

Q: My question is about employees who work for multiple brands. If the employee is an expression of the brand, how do we square that circle in the reality of the multiemployer, multibrand world? There will be more of that, not less.

A: We think the solution lies in values. Our recommendation is to build a values-based and values-driven organization. While the values of organizations are sometimes described differently, they often are ragingly consistent. That should be at the core—the common core of what we ask our people to embrace. We should also encourage people to be lifelong learners so they can become students of the cultures and brands they intersect throughout their careers. Recruit and develop your workforce with these things in mind, then measure and manage these messages and their effectiveness over time.

chapter thirteen | **Seeing Things Differently**

Jay Spach
*Principal, Jay Spach Consulting, Partners in Transformation
and former SVP, Organizational Development, Thomson Reuters*

*For over 18 years, Jay Spach was Senior Vice President,
Organizational Development, at Thomson Reuters. He led
transformations of both the Human Resources and Finance
functions at the Thomson Corporation, ultimately supporting the
acquisition of Reuters in 2008. Jay recently started his own
consulting practice focused on culture change, organization design
and transformation.*

When we asked Jay about the intersection of HR and Marketing
disciplines and how they affect successful organizations, he had an
immediate answer. "It's all about making what looks like something
on the outside actually be that way on the inside. The benefit of this
for successful organizations is that their brand, what they tell the
outside and what they show to the outside, actually comes from
something that is true on the inside. The brand they present to the
world is, in fact, supported by the way their people act and perform
and interact with their colleagues, their customers and with the
outside world."

Jay defines brand quite broadly. "It's what most brand managers
want stakeholders to think about when they think about the brand,
that is, the overall feel, and perception of the company's products,
employees, customer experience and customer service. And brand

is not just what the customer experiences; it's what the whole external world thinks of when it thinks of the company. For example, as a consumer I will probably never be a customer of Caterpillar. Yet I do have a sense of the Caterpillar brand."

Seeing the Brand in Context

To help HR people understand their impact on a company's brand, Jay developed what he calls a Brand Continuum. The graphic on page 118 illustrates the continuum; here's how Jay described it. "The promise that we present to all of our stakeholders starts with our purpose—why we exist, the value we add to our customers. The promise then moves through our values, the things we believe in; and then the behaviors we want to support in our organization. This all gets combined with people and policies in the organization, and, over time, it becomes our culture. And this all plays out for employees in our employee value proposition. Then it gets combined with things like products and customer service and other interactions, and is presented and promised to the external world as our brand."

So what does all this mean for the head of Human Resources? Typically, the CHRO's position could be summed up as: "My job is all about people. The brand—that's Marketing's purview." But if HR people think about brand in the context of Jay's continuum, they would come to a different conclusion. HR has a lot to do with values, behaviors, culture, employee value proposition. That's four of the six elements in the continuum. "I think that's how HR heads need to see things differently, to understand whether they're actually impacting the brand, or helping the organization impact the brand in the way it should. Unfortunately, most HR heads wouldn't list 'brand' as something they have a major impact on."

Brand Continuum

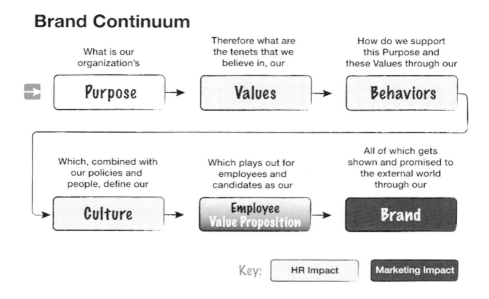

Marketing, on the other hand, is frequently all too aware of the people impact on the brand. "Marketing people spend a lot of time on the company's brand and how to support it, but they're frustrated by the aspects of the brand that are out of their control, which in their mind is pretty much most of it—how employees act and interact with customers. For example, a multimillion dollar airline marketing and brand campaign can be completely squandered by just one flight attendant acting rudely."

Great companies understand the connections between people and brand. "But you can't make those connections if the HR head is oblivious to the impact of employees' behaviors on the brand," said

Jay. "The employee answering the phone is far more 'the brand' than the things we usually associate with brand, like advertising. In fact, if the brand is the promise of the organization, that promise is most immediately felt in customer interactions with Sales, Service and, increasingly, e-commerce."

Working Collaboratively

When HR people see things differently, Jay believes that they will do things differently. And one of the "do different" things is collaborating with Marketing. "Initiating a collaboration is all about finding something that needs to be done that can't be done by either one of them alone. If the Marketing organization identified some specific aspects of employees' behaviors that had a negative impact on the brand, then working with HR around changing that behavior might spark a collaboration. And if the HR organization saw this negative impact, I think they'd want to do something about it together."

HR has a lot to do with the elements that make up the brand.

Jay identified recruiting as an area where the two functions could successfully collaborate. "Marketing can help improve the perception of the brand, so that people will want to come to work for the company. Then HR has the responsibility for ensuring that the experience inside matches the external brand and the recruiting story on the outside," Jay said.

Brand Ambassadors

Not surprisingly, Jay likes the idea of employees acting as brand ambassadors. But not all brand ambassadors are created equal.

Some companies have tried an approach that Jay doesn't think is effective. "Marketing says, 'We ought to have brand ambassadors.' So they have a brand ambassador program. They go out and try to describe the profile and role of a brand ambassador – usually without collaborating with HR – and recruit 5 percent of the sales force to be trained as brand ambassadors. It's hard for me to imagine why you would want one out of 20 salespeople to be brand ambassadors. I think every customer-facing employee has to be a brand ambassador."

Jay gave Disney as an example of the right way to create brand ambassadors. "It's a great brand. We've all read about the training of Disney's customer-facing employees – specifically customer-facing employees in large animal costumes. Disney doesn't say, 'We want you to go to brand ambassador training.' I think the employees learn 'This is what it means to be an employee in a Disney theme park.' And they are all great brand ambassadors. They see it as their job, not just a discrete piece of it. They understand the purpose and the culture of the organization and how that links with the brand and promise of Disney."

Then there's the whole area of social media. "Recruiters are really diving into social networking. There's a Marketing aspect to it, and they're asking Marketing to help them. So there's a door in for Marketing to say to recruiters, 'Yeah, I'll help you with that. By the way, could you help us with the fact that we don't think our salespeople are actually representing the brand very well in some of their interactions?' Another spark, another acknowledgment that maybe they should work together."

In Jay's opinion, success in recruiting talent starts with purpose, the first element in his continuum. "I think all the research tells us, in one form or another, that attracting talent starts with a close connection to the purpose of the organization. An organization that has a clear sense of purpose attracts people who are attracted to that purpose. And organizations that lack a clear sense of purpose have to use other methods to attract people and retain them and grow them. The more employees sense that what they are doing is important, and therefore believe that their behaviors and the promise that they present are important, the more they will connect closely to the organization. Strong cultures keep people. And weak ones—well, they are wide open to the vicissitudes of the job market."

The Next Big Thing

Jay identified another aspect of corporate activity where HR and Marketing, along with Strategy, should be closely aligned. "The next big thing for HR is workforce planning* that comes from the

* For more on strategic workforce planning, see Jeff Joerres, page 25.

company's overall strategy. I think we're just beginning to scratch the surface of what real workforce planning is. To me, it's understanding your workforce in a way that is so deep that you've identified the key jobs you're betting on for the future. What kinds of people can do those jobs? Where are those jobs, demographically, geographically? Where do we need to be in order to source them? That's linking workforce planning to the company's strategy. Then you have to understand how to attract the people you need; that's where Marketing can help. Then you have to know how to keep them, which is where HR plays the lead role."

Jay brought up the issue of how HR heads can become strategic partners. "Business leaders need this kind of workforce planning, whether they know it or not. They need the insights that HR can give them around understanding the current workforce and translating strategic needs into workforce requirements. HR heads need to be out in front, doing just that, so that CEOs won't be asking 'Do I want my HR person to be strategic or not?' They'll just be saying, 'Give me more of that!'"

Ask the Partners

Q: Usually, in any new collaboration attempts, it's the first step that's the most critical. In your experience, what are the first things Marketing does wrong when approached by HR to collaborate? Then what are the first things HR does wrong when approached by Marketing?

A: Each side is likely to react based on preconceived notions of the other function. Marketing people sometimes have a very narrow view of what HR does, dismissing their work as administrative and internally focused. HR people may perceive that marketers are more concerned with style than substance and wonder why they get all the attention. As a result, each party is likely to react in "turf" protection mode, feeling the need to control the interaction and the intersection between the two disciplines.

Our advice to both parties is to approach the relationship as a true partnership. Consider what the other party brings to the partnership that complements your function's skills, knowledge and abilities.

For HR, Marketing can bring creativity: new ways to look at things (including "old" problems and obstacles), as well as energy and outside perspective.

For Marketing, HR brings discipline and processes to improve effectiveness, along with internal legitimacy and "weightiness" for many of the ideas.

Working in partnership, the team can broaden marketing channels, inspire brand ambassadorship to take root, and increase employee loyalty and commitment.

chapter fourteen | **Standing Shoulder to Shoulder**

Len Vickers
VP, Marketing for GE and Xerox (retired)

Len Vickers started his career as a product/brand manager for Unilever in his native England. He came to the United States in the mid-'60s to work on Madison Avenue. A decade later, Jack Welch hired him as Marketing Executive for GE's Consumer Sector; he later became Vice President of Corporate Marketing. During his GE tenure, Len was named both Marketing and Advertising Person of the Year. (CEO Jeff Immelt's first job at GE was in the Marketing Consulting Group, which reported up to Len.) From 1989 to 1996, Len was Senior Vice President, Worldwide Marketing, for Xerox Corporation. He recently retired as head of Vickers Associates, a New York-based business consultancy focused on helping companies with their vision, strategic marketing and repositioning.

Len Vickers started his career in American advertising during the heyday of the "Mad Men" era. At GE, he helped create one of the most enduring ad campaigns of the 20th century, "We bring good things to life." In the mid-'90s he positioned Xerox as *The Document Company*. Len shared some of his history and a unique view on how Chief HR and Marketing Officers should join forces.

Drop, Keep, Add

Len believes in the wisdom of Peter Drucker when he said, "Above all, abandonment is the key to innovation – both because it frees the necessary resources and because it stimulates the search for the new that will replace the old." Len's shorthand version is *Drop, Keep, Add*:

- Drop what isn't working,
- Keep and improve what is working, and
- Add new and innovative products and services to refresh the brand, stimulate organic growth and increase revenue.

As Len sees it, "Quality and productivity have to do with eliminating waste. On the one hand you're taking cost down; you're taking out waste and re-work. That's the abandonment, that's the freeing up. Then you start doing innovative things that deliver on what you stand for, that revitalize the brand, that will grow revenue. You have to do both. *Drop* and *keep* have to do with quality and productivity. And the *add* has to do with organic growth, with revenues.

"Now you can't do that with an insecure workforce. People who are worried about losing their jobs are going to freeze. You don't free up; you can't move on. It's about freeing up trapped resources and making the workforce secure enough to focus on the new. All in the context of what you stand for, your brand."

A Brief History of Marketing, Advertising and Brand

When Jack Welch was head of GE's Consumer Sector, he hired Len Vickers to create better marketing and advertising as part of GE's "marketing renaissance." Reg Jones, who preceded Welch as CEO, was tired of the company's image being hurt by major appliance advertising that focused on promoting deep discount days. For his part, Welch wanted to restore some of the luster he thought Marketing had lost since his early days at GE. Welch described Marketing as having been "pushed down the corridor, away from the general manager," in favor of the emerging discipline of Strategic Planning, which GE invented. In addition to restoring some of Marketing's pre-eminence, Welch wanted true *consumer* marketing, sensing that GE really hadn't done that.

As Len recalled, "GE had written the book on Marketing, postwar and into the '50s and '60s. I think they actually defined Marketing— Marketing as opposed to Sales. Focusing on problems and solutions, not just products. They defined Marketing. For me, then and now, Marketing means leading people to what they will *learn* to want—not just what they ardently desire at the time." Len offered Apple as an example of a company that has succeeded in leading people to want its innovative products.

Working for Welch at the end of the '70s, Len helped create the familiar "We bring good things to life" campaign for GE. "What I was responsible for at GE was mainly an advertising idea. Now, it implied innovation. It meant innovation in a very human way, on a human scale. I would say, with hindsight, an advertising classic. It lasted 25 years. Very successful." [Authors' note: GE's "We bring good things to life" didn't make *Advertising Age's* "Top 10 Advertising Slogans of the Century"—but it *was* one of five Honorable Mentions.]

"After I'd been at GE about a year, I had to pitch the new campaign to Reg Jones. I remember my opening sentence, and I sensed I had him. Jones was a financial guy, and my opening sentence was, 'Brand image is our least tangible, most valuable asset.' In business as in life, I think intangibles are very important—usually all important. The dictum that 'you can only manage what you can measure' is a deathtrap in business, education and politics."

Brand, a notion that's ubiquitous, almost overused today, was a relatively new concept at the time. "Brand, as a word, wasn't really used at GE when I joined," said Len. Long before everyone had a personal brand, Len was working on his definition. "Basically, I break it down to 'What do you stand for?' It's not simply whether you have a high profile; it's what you stand for. You have to put meaning into brand to make it useful, to say what brand is. You can say it's reputation, identity, trademark." Len sees brand, what you stand for, as an overarching idea. "Feeding into what you stand for are your people, products and services, and communications. Very often services *are* your people. Ultimately, everything a company does speaks."

Nowadays people talk about branding all the time. But it's something that's easier said than done. "I do want to stress the difficulty of branding and how obsessive it should be. Words matter. Images matter. Tone matters. It's important to get the position right, to get the language right. It's not trivial. And to know when you're putting the pitch before the product. Sometimes you have to do that, although Winston Churchill cautioned against it." And then Len quoted Churchill from memory: "'In public affairs, it's wiser to avoid prophesying beforehand, because it's much better policy to prophesy after the event has taken place.'"

Len's tenure at GE predated the era of employer branding as we know it today. "But they were very conscious of their reputation as a well-managed company. They had that self-image. They may not have used 'brand,' but they certainly understood the concept of reputation. Just as Warren Buffet does now. He's not afraid of losses; what he fears is loss of reputation. I think Reg Jones or Jack Welch would have said the same thing."

Along with reputation, GE was very mindful of hi-pots/talent. In fact, one of GE's three well-established processes, along with Strategic Planning (five-year outlook) and Operational/Tactical Planning (one-year outlook), was an HR process focused on high-potential development. "They may not have used the word *talent*," said Len, "but they were very much on to the concept. They had a serious, authentic process to assess high-potential employees and develop them for leadership roles."

HR and Marketing

While he was at Xerox, Len worked closely with HR, particularly the training organization. He was a frequent speaker at leadership development courses, sharing *The Document Company* positioning. We asked what advice would he offer to HR heads to enable them to see their roles in the context of their company's brand. He responded with a vivid metaphor. (See the illustration below.)

"I don't see a face-to-face discussion between HR and Marketing. I see a shoulder-to-shoulder dialogue. You don't accomplish much when you're face to face. It should be shoulder to shoulder looking at something. And what you're looking at is an honest-to-God reappraisal of the workplace, on the one hand; and the marketplace on the other. Those are the two essential contexts you have to look at. What's happening in our workplace? And what's happening in our marketplace? What you're trying to do is to really figure out what you can do in both arenas to get aligned, get integrated, get focused on becoming who we are, becoming what we want to stand for."

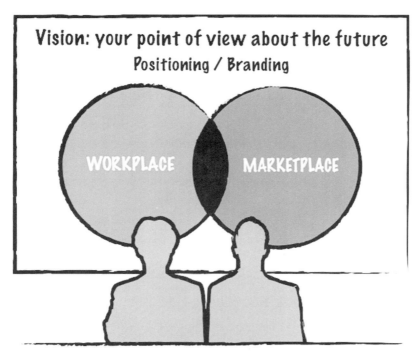

Len continued with his metaphor. "I know people are very turf conscious. That's why I used the phrase 'shoulder to shoulder' rather than 'face to face.' It's not a negotiation. If you're into face to face, it's a negotiation. It's all about winning and losing. It doesn't work; you've already lost. Literally, some of the best conversations I've had were when I was jogging with someone. And with my kids, driving them in the car. There's something about the shared experience where you're both looking ahead. You're doing something together. It's a good image, a metaphor that works."

Part of the analysis of workplace must address what makes people want to join and stay with a company. For Len it comes down to recognition. "There is a deep human need to be seen, to be recognized. You've got to start there; that's the beginning of everything. People want to make a difference in their own ways. They want to be rewarded—and it's not just financial rewards. They want to be thanked and praised. And if they're not doing a good job, that should be acknowledged. I'm all for candor and honesty and telling people the truth. But you need people who are honest enough, tough enough and strong enough to do it."

I see HR and Marketing in a shoulder-to-shoulder dialogue.

Len recalled his own days working for Welch. "Life was a running appraisal with Jack Welch. You knew where you stood every day, whether you were a prince or a pig—in those words. You got instant feedback—good job, bad job. It's just a question of being candid with people. It requires a lot of spine."

The Power of the Overheard Message

Len is a big fan of what he calls the *overheard message*: sharing with employees advertising and other communications developed for an external audience.

As part of launching the "We bring good things to life" campaign, Jack Welch asked Len to do a road show to share the positioning and advertising with employees—something unheard of at the time. "We spent a fortune, temporarily shutting down production at factories in Cleveland, Louisville, Syracuse, Schenectady, Bridgeport so employees could attend the presentation. I put together a show on what GE stands for, and people were so proud. It was a superb campaign. When I played the commercials to those employee audiences, I could feel the impact. I actually felt the impact of the emotion in the audience. Because they identified with it. And it made them feel good. People want to feel part of something bigger. It really, really, really worked.

"It was Welch's idea. And my God, did it have a payoff. It really had a payoff. There's no question that the road show, together with great results, helped Jack get the CEO job. People loved seeing the advertising. And that's what I call the power of the overheard message. The external message has impact inside."

Ask the Partners

Q: Why did you want to write this book? What deep need do you see? What opportunity do you feel?

A: We experienced first hand the power of the partnership between HR and Marketing. For HR, it's a plus for attracting and retaining talent; and good for the brand on the Marketing side. Recognizing that this was not a common experience in the broader HR community, we realized that this was a story worth sharing.

Our collaboration was a natural, since we've worked together for many years. We chose to reach out to thought leaders in the HR community for their input and to see where that might lead us. We quickly understood that there is a big appetite and considerable energy around this subject matter. People are energized by the possibilities. They want to share their stories and learn from each other. Like you—and probably most marketers—we appreciate the power of personal stories to communicate. That's why we opted for interviews and a conversational style, to allow our contributors to tell their stories in their own words.

We want to provide HR and Marketing people the opportunity to keep the conversation going and foster the formation of a community where people can continue to share their stories and experiences. Our hope is that our efforts enrich both disciplines and those who practice them.

chapter fifteen | **Creating a Level Playing Field for Talent**

John Daniels
Chairman, Quarles & Brady LLP

Quarles & Brady provides client-centric, national-level legal services from its integrated network of regional offices across the United States and in Shanghai, China. The firm applies a solutions-oriented approach to complicated legal problems for its clients among major corporations, government agencies and nonprofits as well as individuals. Quarles has earned a reputation for client service and attributes its success to the strength of its deep relationships.

John Daniels has been chair of the firm since 2007, during which time Law Dragon *named him a premier national law firm leader, and the* National Law Journal *named him one of its "50 most influential minority lawyers in America." During his tenure, John has focused his efforts on transforming the firm into a client-focused, business-driven organization, evolving out of the traditional, reactive model that has characterized the industry in the past.*

A self-professed sports fan, John Daniels has had the good fortune to represent several major athletes (who happen to have an instinct for business) during his career. The ones who have been most successful, John notes, have tended to speak with conspicuous pride about their teams instead of themselves. "They talked about those organizations as having elevated them, lifting them above whatever level of ability they already had, providing them with the capacity to perform at an even higher level."

It's clear that John shares those athlete-clients' beliefs in the transformative power of organizations, suggesting, "When people believe in the organization and commit themselves to its success rather than their own, the chances of accomplishing superior achievements multiply, and then success breeds yet more success, including that which reflects back on each individual. And when people feel strongly connected to an organization, they're proud to talk about it with others, which brings more people together in pursuit of common goals, expanding the effect geometrically."

John's belief in the organization has shaped his game plan for Quarles & Brady. The firm's strategy is a vision of collective effort, driven by four key planks:

- Unwavering focus on the client.
- Commitment to diversity.
- Team-based talent development.
- Supporting a greater good.

Focus on the Client

The client is the polestar of any successful firm, but Quarles & Brady postulates that it actually *exists* to solve problems and create value for its clients.

That focus also defines what "talent" means to the firm's recruiters. They recognize that newly minted lawyers do not spring out of law school with the judgment, talent and aptitude to solve complex problems, let alone with a client-centric, organizationally driven view of success. There are several characteristics that he looks for in nascent lawyers—traits that he believes correlate with long-term success in the legal profession.

Integrity tops the list. As John explained, "There's always a short-cut way of pursuing things, but you have to start off, right from the beginning in the profession, with an appreciation for the notion of, 'There's a way that *we* conduct business.' As people are working on projects, we want them to understand that what they're doing is going to affect someone's life. We want them to embrace every assignment completely, as though they were doing it for someone in their own family, and in a way that they would be comfortable explaining everything they did. It's just a core value that you want to have in your organization." John sets an unwavering standard for all Quarles & Brady employees from their hire dates, making them understand that the firm has "zero tolerance for anything that would in any way suggest less than the highest standard of integrity is acceptable."

When people feel strongly connected to an organization, they're proud to talk about it.

Next in importance is what John calls an "instinct for service." Some people derive a deep and personal sense of satisfaction from providing service to others, while others see it as a bother; in John's view, the latter aren't cut out to be lawyers. People who appreciate and recognize implicit value in service to others have a much better chance of sustaining a legal career.

Handling complex issues further requires lawyers to be expert communicators, and it's not just a matter of effective speaking and writing. Excellence in communications most critically demands truly exceptional listening skills. John says, "In an effective dialogue with the client, you listen carefully in order to peel back the layers and get to the essence of what the client *really* wants to solve. If you don't grasp what the client is fundamentally trying to achieve, you may provide an adequate legal response, but you won't necessarily advance the interests of the client as effectively as you might have done, given deeper insight. Superior value comes from giving the client exactly what they want, even when they don't clearly ask for it."

John recently chaired a panel of global general counsels—lawyers who are handling some of today's most complex legal issues, for some of the most complex business operations. As part of his preparation, he met with each of them and asked what they valued most in dealing with outside law firms. "Almost to a person," John recounted, "they desire a deeper level of communication with their lawyers."

Finally, John believes that lawyers need a degree of flexibility to properly serve their clients. In a competitive environment, fraught with complex issues and adversarial situations, there are always unknowns and variables. "Lawyers need resilience," John said, "so if there's a jog in the path, they don't lose focus on where they're going. They bounce back and continue to provide the best advice."

Commitment to Diversity

John and his firm are committed to diversity because it is essential to recruiting the best talent. The kind of diversity that Quarles & Brady has created isn't the formulaic, check-the-box variety—that approach leaves some people feeling like winners and others like losers. For John, diversity isn't an artificial mandate, but rather a part of the culture and the way work gets done.

"Diversity, to me, is a mindset in which you can be comfortable discussing things that are outside your own background, and where you don't make assumptions about other people's abilities. When people become part of an organization, one of the most important things they can do is perceive and explore viewpoints that don't come naturally from their backgrounds. In doing so, they communicate different perspectives to one another instead of making assumptions about the beliefs and conduct of others, generating more solutions to choose from. Very quickly they come to understand that, in fact, it's highly beneficial to have access to those diverse skills and knowledge."

John recalls an incident that occurred more than 35 years ago, early in his career. At that time there were few diverse lawyers in major law firms. "By training, I was a real estate and business lawyer. My law firm was handling a major, major deal, and I was working with a tax lawyer from another very fine firm. He later told me that he had never worked with an African-American lawyer on a complex business deal and admitted that he assumed I didn't have the same level of expertise in tax that he did. In fact, tax was something that I had a natural affinity for, and I had aced my tax courses at Harvard

Law School. On that deal, he lost the benefit of what I had to contribute, and so did his client. When there's a lack of organizational diversity, people sometimes make those kinds of assumptions, and some don't even recognize the value that has been lost."

Happily for John (and the firm's clientele), the talent pool today is much more diverse. For John, the key to creating a diverse law firm is a laser-like concentration on *talent*. "I think that sometimes people don't focus on the real essence of talent," he says. "Too often they get distracted by personal biases, which robs them of the capacity to recognize and take advantage of talent. If you can really stay focused on getting the best talent without those distractions, it gives you a huge competitive advantage. At Quarles, we want people to know that they're going to be judged solely on the basis of talent. That's a pretty compelling idea for most people, and it's important to everyone, whether or not they happen to be diverse."

Quarles & Brady fosters diversity of thought as well. "I always like to ask everybody in the organization if they can think of better ways to serve our clients. If you simply look for all of the ideas to flow from the top, you won't enjoy the benefit of diversity of thought. Realistically, when you step back and think about where the best ideas come from, it's not at all predictable, let alone reasonable, to expect them all to come from the executive level."

For example, when John solicited ideas for organizational improvement during a recent partner meeting, he received more than 100 suggestions; then, asking the general staff generated another 100 ideas or so. John got a lot of conventional ideas from people who have probably done things a certain way for a long time. Meanwhile, many of the ideas from associates and the administrative staff were excellent suggestions that John realized weren't likely to have come from even the most innovative and successful partners. "When you have newer and younger employees who aren't quite as convinced that the current way is the right way, you get some really good ideas that are very productive. And when you share those ideas across the organization, other people usually recognize them as good ones and accept them."

Team-based Talent Development

Like Dick Antoine (see page 61) and the majority of HR professionals, John recognizes that most talent development takes place on the job, especially with respect to challenging assignments. Considering the preponderance of new and emerging legal challenges in today's business world, there's no shortage of development opportunities for Quarles & Brady lawyers. "Not surprisingly, our approach to talent development is collaborative—a team approach," said John. "We work a lot on a notion of taking the best talent in the firm and molding it to get the right result for the client. I think our lawyers are better able to deliver service because they match their skills with other team members who complement them and get to the right results together."

In John's experience, "Everybody comes to an environment with a certain set of experiences. They see the world in part through those experiences, and they tend to overemphasize the skills in which they're really strong and underemphasize the areas in which they're really weak." Working in teams serves to shift those perceptions and eliminate inadequacies. John observes that lawyers working on a team are less likely to be certain about things that may seem obvious on the surface but which may require different reactions when viewed from multiple perspectives. A good mix of skills on the team leads it to dig beneath the surface and approach work more thoughtfully and with an open mind. Once again, that dynamic works to the best interests of both the team and the client.

Supporting a Greater Good

Working with Will and the Versant staff, Quarles & Brady recently produced a video highlighting the firm's commitment to corporate social responsibility. John recognizes that clients don't generally select a law firm on the basis of its *pro bono* work and community support. "But those commitments reaffirm their view of how you operate as an organization. It's about believing that your organization is something more than computers and law libraries."

And it's a source of pride, a sense of connection for the firm's employees. As John sees it, that connection is part of the transformative power of organizations.

Everybody Counts, Every Day

John's motto at Quarles & Brady is "Everybody counts, every day." It's a commitment that all 1,000 people working at Quarles understand is fundamental to how the firm operates. As he explains, "What's implicit in that phrase is that everyone in the organization should feel a sense of ownership and pride in their firm. They should feel that it's more than just a job, and that we're more than just a law firm. Really great enterprises create that belief in people, and it is evident in everything they do."

Ask the Partners

Q: Organizations have performance goals and metrics. When the organization's performance falls short, there are typically two schools of thought: People who want to accentuate the shortcomings, and on the other hand, those who don't want to face them. How do you put things in place to make sure that you're navigating the right course between those two perspectives? How do you communicate and deal with people when you have a result that is not what you would expect or want?

A: We think the right course is not either to accentuate or ignore, but to address the situation in the right context. First, you need alignment in goal setting. If you simply set functional goals that are divorced from the business goals, you allow for equivocation when goals are missed. We believe that you have to take great care in setting meaningful goals (meaningful to the business) for functional partners and hold everyone accountable for delivering them. Tie individual and functional goals to client and market expectations as well as the business goals to drive alignment and organizational success. Communicate how these relate to and support one another so that individuals and groups clearly understand their responsibilities for and ability to impact the business goals.

Follow through by rewarding the organization for achieving the stated goals and specifically the functional partners for their leadership. If the goals aren't achieved, then honest, objective feedback is required. As with all constructive feedback, the goal is improved performance during the next cycle.

chapter sixteen | **Learning to Manage and Lead**

Rose Fass
Founder & CEO, fassforward consulting group

"Companies that don't like consulting firms hire us." That's the way fassforward presents itself to potential clients on its Web site. In the ten years since she founded her company in Westchester County, New York, Rose and British colleague, Gavin McMahon, McMahon Consulting, have worked with executive teams from Fortune *500 companies to enable them to face tough challenges, solve complex problems, execute their strategies and deliver bottom-line results. Leadership development is also a sweet spot for fassforward. Rose and Gavin also have a proven track record in developing leaders for senior-level positions.*

fassforward is a company of dyads, which the dictionary defines as groups of two people in an ongoing interaction. Rose and Gavin were the original dyad and ultimately became the prototype. They were male and female, left-brained and right-brained, of different generations and from different countries and cultural backgrounds. They were, in fact, complementary. They balanced each other and discovered that they worked very effectively together. That insight shaped fassforward's hiring strategy going forward.

In a service business like fassforward, people are critical; they *are* your product. Virtually all client work is handled by dyads based on pairing complementary skills, backgrounds and thinking styles, as well as characteristics like gender and ethnicity. As a result, fassforward is a company as diverse as the companies they work with. More important, that diversity fits with the kind of work fassforward does. "When you have a group of people who all operate the same way and have a very generic point of view, it's difficult to drive change or do things differently," Rose said.

Branding from the Inside

fassforward hired more dyads and grew so quickly that Rose and Gavin didn't spend a great deal of time up front trying to brand themselves. As the group expanded, they saw the lack of brand as a gap. "We didn't feel we had a really well-articulated brand, so that our people could go to a cocktail party and be brand ambassadors who could have a conversation about what we do in a very clear, concise way. We're a service, with an intangible product. It's not so easy to get your arms around it."

At that point, fassforward consulting group had reached a size, both in terms of people and clients, that Rose brought in a Chief Operating Officer to help manage the business and a Chief Growth Officer to develop the brand. Their first task was to create a plan and process for pulling people into the brand. "We called an all-company meeting—about 20 employees—and we started by asking them to describe what _they_ saw as the brand. The right-brained people drew pictures and wrote stories; the left-brained used diagrams and data." Synthesizing the input, just as they might do with a client, they identified "vision" as a common theme. And the group came up with:

*"fassforward has the uncanny ability to bring
a vision to game-changing reality."*

As Rose explained, "That's become a big part of the brand. Our employees are now able to have those conversations, and we've actually gotten a couple of employee referrals, so we're seeing it start to work. We have more work to do in this area, but I think we've made a good start."

A significant part of fassforward's work is delivering an executive development program for one of its major clients, a *Fortune* 50 company. The program has been a success since it launched six years ago. Every member of that "freshman" class is now in a C-level position, running a major line of business or responsible for a significant geographical area. The program covers both management and leadership skills. "We make distinctions, as many companies do, between good, sound management practice on the one hand and leadership on the other. Management is the doing; it's about operational strategy and execution, all the things that are about what employees do day to day. Then we spend a good deal of time on leadership, which is about: 'Who I am. And how who I am impacts my people and their results.' And we say both things are important. To be effective, you have to manage *and* lead."

Managing with Message Discipline

Message discipline is the term Rose and Gavin coined to convey the importance of words. "I think you have to be very disciplined about what you say, how you say it, who you say it to and when you say it. The simpler you keep the language, the less apt you are to confuse people. And the less apt you are to contradict yourself."

When we asked why people don't use simple language, Rose replied, "Sometimes it's because they think they don't sound important enough if they don't use multisyllabic words. But sometimes I think it's because they don't know fully what they want to convey. They basically obscure the message by just sounding smart. Getting people to distill what they want to say to its essence and putting it out there changes things."

The simpler you keep the language,
the less apt you are to confuse people.

The focus on message discipline grew out of a familiar complaint fassforward was hearing from virtually all their clients: "We've got a great strategy. I wish I could get my people to execute on it." This was often followed by the comment, "They just don't get it."

Rose pushed back. "If the masses 'don't get it,' who owns that? The leader owns that." And as she peeled back the layers, she challenged her clients by saying, "If execution and operational discipline are so critical to you, you need to understand that they're driven by message discipline. You need to put those two things together: 'Message discipline drives operational discipline.' When employees get multiple messages—from headquarters, from region, from their boss, each with a slightly different spin, they don't know what to pay attention to anymore."

To clear up the confusion, the team at fassforward advises their clients to figure out the common thread on how to convey the message in such a simple way that everyone understands what's being asked of them. "That doesn't mean the same message that's said at the corporate level has to be said all the way down in the same exact way," Rose said. "Rather, it has to be translated at each level in a way that everybody gets it."

Rose gave the example of a series of strategic imperatives that one of her client companies had developed. These made perfect sense to people at senior levels. But those same messages didn't convey much meaning to sales reps. The table below illustrates what can happen if managers simply parrot the same messages to all levels in the organization.

What Happens When Managers Simply "Communicate"

Strategic Imperative	What it meant to Senior Leaders	What it meant to Sales Reps
Widen the revenue lead	We're leading our competitors, but we don't have enough of a jump on them; we need to make the lead bigger.	Huh?
Reduce churn	We're losing too many customers.	Huh?
Lean in profitability	We need to improve our PE ratio (price to earnings).	Uh oh. I get that one; it means cost cutting.

Managers believe their job is to communicate, but Rose begs to differ. "fassforward has taken a very strong stand on this and said, 'No, it's not. It's every manager/leader's job to _translate_. You have an absolute responsibility to translate the messages you're getting

148

from the top through to your employees so that their interpretation is both consistent with the direction of the company and meaningful to them. And if it isn't, it's not because they don't get it. It's because you don't get it.'"

Working with a group of sales managers, Rose coached them through the task of translating the corporate messages into clear terms that sales reps could both understand and act on. "And they were like, 'Wow. This really hits home.' So you take each message and you bring it all the way down so that it matters significantly to the employee." The table below shows how much more meaningful the translated messages were to sales reps.

What Happens When Managers Translate Messages

Strategic Imperative	Translated for Sales Reps
Widen the revenue lead	**Earn more dollars** • More revenue dollars for the company • More commission dollars for you • And work to really earn those dollars from your customers because they don't owe it to you
Reduce churn	It's all about your customers: **Get 'em and keep 'em**
Lean in profitability	**Do the right thing** • The right thing for you • The right thing for the company • And above all, the right thing for the customer

"So we ended up with a very simple, distilled message that's now pervasive throughout the company. No one forgets it. It doesn't have to be on a laminated card. People don't have to sit and think about what they've been told to do. That's just one example of message discipline that drives what you want people to do and how you get to operational discipline," Rose summarized.

149

The Shadow of the Leader

Business bookshelves abound with volumes on "Level 5" leaders and charismatic leaders and participative leaders. "We don't think that any one type of leader is necessarily better than another," said Rose. "We believe that whatever kind of leader you are, you need to use that to your greatest advantage and make sure that you are aware of any blind spots that could impair your leadership. So we spend a lot of time helping people understand, 'If you're this type of leader, how is that going to work for you? And what are the things that aren't going to work for you?'* One of the early CEO sponsors of our program coined the phrase 'the shadow of the leader.' We've adopted that and use it in all our programs for that client. We encourage participants to ask themselves, 'What shadow am I casting?'"

A critical point that Rose emphasizes is that "leadership happens in the conversation." She challenges leadership program participants to ask themselves, "What are the conversations you're having with your people? Do they line up with the messages you've put out there?" Those conversations take on great importance. "When you become a leader, it's difficult to have casual conversations. 'Casual' in this instance doesn't mean 'friendly.' It means that you can't be casual about the things you say."

Rose gave the example of a senior leader who was creating a new role in his organization. He had mentioned this in passing when

---

* This is very similar to the way Stu Kantor approaches executive coaching; see
  page 154.

speaking with a member of his team, leaving that individual with the clear impression that he was in line for the new position. Then in an executive meeting later that day, he learned about changes from the top and realized that there were other candidates that he should consider. "Unfortunately, the leader had a 'casual' conversation he's going to have to unhook from if he decides to go in a different direction. And that's a problem he could have easily avoided," said Rose. "This is the kind of thing we spend a lot of time on with the leaders we're developing."

Another pitfall for leaders to avoid: "The last one who talks to me wins." Rose acknowledged it's all too easy for leaders to fall into this trap. "Someone will come up to the leader with a problem or an issue, and they immediately go into a fix-it mode, before they've had a chance to test the waters, to find out what's really going on. We advise them to be very careful that the last person who speaks to them isn't the last word on what needs to happen," said Rose.

"We want our clients and people in our programs to understand that leadership, in and of itself, is a practice—like engineering or accounting or the law. And if you're in a leadership role, you have to hone that practice. You need to spend time on it if you want to become a better leader."

Don't Burn Bridges

Rose closed our interview by sharing some personal advice. "People don't necessarily appreciate that the bridges they create during their careers can become incredibly important; especially in this economy. If you find yourself out of your company for the right or wrong reasons, you want to know that you have people you can call. I see people burn bridges all the time. Then when they're out of a job, there's no one to call. Be there for people, because they're going to be there for you."

"Walking Around Decks": An Unexpected Product

"Our people are unique," said Rose. "We give them a lot of room to think on their own and be creative. And because of that, they come up with ideas that we couldn't even imagine, and they turned those ideas into valuable new products. Our people have become very much a part of what we end up offering as a consulting firm, expanding on what we originally started out to do."

Client requests prompted one such offering. "We heard very senior leaders say, 'I have an idea I want to get across. But if it looks like I have it all worked out, I'll get a lot of resistance. But I don't want to go with just a napkin-sketch outline because that will lead people to conclude I haven't given the idea much thought.' A couple of our people said, 'Why don't we put together something that's hand drawn, that looks like doodling but hangs together and reflects some real thinking behind it.' Then Gavin said, 'That's the kind of deck they could walk around with.'

"And that's what we call them: walking around decks. It's a way for a client to tee up an idea with other leaders in their company, a visual starting point for a friendly conversation. It doesn't look stilted or formal. But it's extremely clever and well put together. And our clients love them. It's become a niche business for us."

Ask the Partners

Q: How much of the message you have around employer branding and its importance is being packaged for C-level executives to pay attention to? They're focused on "How do I get my employees to do the right things—what I need them to do, at all levels of the company?" I don't know what they're thinking about it as employer branding. I think this is a huge opportunity.

A: We agree with your assessment. Our recommendation is to help executives connect the dots; don't assume they will take the time to do it themselves. And be explicit. Often there are too many messages and too much clutter. So the important gets drowned out by the urgent or the immediate crisis. Identify ways to communicate and reinforce the power of alignment on a regular basis. Finally, make sure that the messages are clear and true.

chapter seventeen | **Helping Leaders Bring out the Best in Others**

Stu Kantor
Principal, Kantor Consulting Associates

Stu Kantor holds a B.A. in Psychology from the University of Michigan and a Ph.D. from Case Western Reserve University. As part of his professional training, he participated in a two-year fellowship at the Menninger Foundation in Topeka, Kansas, and he received a Certificate in Psychoanalysis from the William Alanson White Institute in New York City. Stu began his career working as a clinical psychologist. He has held faculty positions at Columbia University and the City University of New York. In addition, Stu lectures and writes on the role of emotional intelligence in organizations. At this stage in his career, Stu's work is focused on helping people and organizations change. Based in Armonk, New York, he provides one-on-one coaching for senior executives, primarily in the New York metropolitan area. His goal is to help leaders improve their leadership effectiveness by understanding their impact on the people around them.

Virtually everyone we interviewed for this book talked about talent. Most of them see talent from inside the company, as senior leaders or functional heads of HR or Marketing. Stu offers a unique perspective on talent and leadership development. As a consultant, he brings objectivity and, with his psychology background, a deep understanding of what makes effective leaders. Through his one-on-one relationships with senior executives, he provides insight and expertise that no internal mentor, line manager or talent management system can offer.

"All leaders, even great leaders, have relative weaknesses," said Stu. "What really differentiates great leaders from good leaders is their ability to help the people around them to function at their highest level of potential. Self-awareness is a key ingredient of maximizing one's leadership contribution. It's very hard for leaders to connect with and understand the people who work for them if they don't understand themselves and their impact on others so what I do is give people deep, honest feedback about how other people experience working with them. Then I share that with them in a way that allows them to identify the key things that they could do better."

In his work, Stu relies on the concept of emotional intelligence as a framework for self-awareness. "I'm a great believer that emotional intelligence can make a huge difference in the way people are able to pursue their business goals. It's a competency model that enables leaders to recognize that the way they interact with other people can be broken down into tangible and specific component parts. That awareness allows them to identify strengths and weaknesses at their leadership level, and then to work on specific and pragmatic things that make them better leaders.

"For leaders, the impact of what they say and do takes on much greater significance," Stu continued. "So leaders have to be up for the challenge of that responsibility. Senior leaders can't walk down the hallway without knowing that even the _way_ they walk down the hallway has great impact on the people who are observing them." That echoes a similar observation leadership developer Rose Fass (see page 144) offered: "Once you become a leader, no conversation is casual. You can't be casual about the things you say."

A Case Study

Stu's work with one of his current clients illustrates his processes around data collection, feedback and coaching. In her mid-30s, Nancy* has worked for the same multinational employer since earning her MBA ten years ago. She has held a number of positions in Finance and had major roles in several special project assignments, the most important of which was a major acquisition for the company. Based on her consistently superior performance and strong work ethic, Nancy's managers and the Chief Human Resource Officer have identified her as a key talent. They believe that she has the "right stuff" to become a general manager and, ultimately, even the potential to rise to a "C-level" position.

From a development standpoint, what Nancy needed most was experience leading a function. Coincidentally, the head of Investor Relations (IR) was about to retire. Nancy was not necessarily a natural fit for the position. First, IR is outside her domain expertise. Although she has the financial acumen for the job, she lacks experience in communications and interactions with Wall Street and the company's Board of Directors. Second, there was a qualified candidate within the function, although this individual did not have

---

* The name of this client and the details of her situation have been changed to protect her identity.

the same long-term potential as Nancy. Finally, bringing in an outsider could lead to resentment from members of the IR team. On the plus side, Nancy did have experience in the Treasury group, working with bankers and rating agencies, which required related skills. And the timing was perfect.

Ultimately, Nancy was named to the IR position, but not without critical support from the CFO. It was in everyone's best interests that she succeed in the assignment. Her internal mentor would continue to work with her. And the company engaged Stu as her coach. "My job, as an executive development coach," said Stu, "is mostly focused on helping people understand their impact on other people. It's very hard for a leader to connect with and understand the people who work for them if they don't understand themselves."

To provide that understanding, Stu conducted personal interviews with about a dozen people—including Nancy's past and current immediate managers, her mentor, peers and new direct reports. Stu's skill comes into play as he distills the data from his interviews. "My clients hear the themes—the two or three most important development opportunities are usually addressed in a personal way, in a slightly different way from person to person, by about two-thirds of the individuals I interview."

We asked Stu how his clients react to the direct, honest and constructive feedback he provides. "There's a wide range of responses," he replied. "But I'm working with people in the top 100 or so in an organization, people who are privileged enough for the company to spend money to provide this executive development opportunity. Occasionally some people become a little defensive.

But by and large, these are very bright people interested in understanding how they can be better leaders. They appreciate the opportunity to receive this kind of deep, personal, individual executive development. I think it gives them a leg up on somebody who's unaware of their impact on other people."

What about surprises? Does any of Stu's feedback come as a surprise to his clients? "The process I conduct allows the people I coach to hold up the mirror and see their individual strengths and weaknesses as other people experience them," he responded. "And often that includes a couple of surprises. But it isn't usually a radical concept that the individual is presented with. We tend to focus on the themes."

Great leaders help the people around them function at their highest level of potential.

A major theme in Nancy's case is a relatively common one: how to go from being a terrific individual contributor to understanding that there's now too much on her plate for her to tackle everything by herself. The circumstances, however, were somewhat atypical. Most of the time, Stu explained, people rise up through the ranks of a function and then have the opportunity to learn leadership responsibilities within their domain expertise. It's much less frequent that an individual takes on their first leadership responsibly in a new domain. But anyone who aspires to a general management position will ultimately have to move into new areas of expertise.

The feedback confirmed that there was quite a bit of resentment in the organization that Nancy was given this very senior role, clearly a consequence of others believing they understood more about Investor Relations than she did. Stu's advice was "to bring out the best in each of the people who report to her so that she can lead this function with skill and emotional intelligence." For the first time in her career, she will have to delegate and demonstrate her trust in her team members.

Stu also advised Nancy to build on her considerable interpersonal skills by becoming more vocal. "Right now, Nancy is much more comfortable on a one-to-one basis. In a small group, she's the kind of person who really only shares her point of view when it adds something new and different to the conversation. But a leader has more responsibility than just saying something new and different. The leader needs to manage the mood of the group, make sure all the priorities are covered. She needs to weigh in to share her point of view, even if what she has to say is redundant. People need to understand what matters most to her and where she's guiding the group as a whole."

With Stu's coaching and guidance, Nancy is practicing her new leadership skills and achieving positive results. Members of the IR team have been impressed with her general smarts, her integrity and her phenomenal work ethic. It looks like the stretch assignment will be a win-win, for Nancy and the company. "My help will be just a little bit of grease on the wheels for her," Stu remarked. "I think it will help her better understand how people are experiencing her. She's come to understand that she needs to work on being a little bit of a louder voice in public forums, as opposed to the quiet, behind-the-scenes, get-it-done-person she's been. A real TEAM leader, not just a fabulous project manager."

Talent Retention

Like Dick Antoine (see page 61), Stu understands that personal development and stretch assignments can be powerful tools for retaining key talent. "The opportunity to come to know themselves more deeply and pragmatically is very appealing to most individuals who have a long runway. They're eager to understand their impact on other people and to take on additional leadership responsibility," said Stu.

The kind of coaching that Stu provides is obviously a scarce commodity. He advises companies to be highly selective in identifying candidates for this kind of leadership development, warning against a possible "Gresham's Law" effect that could devalue the experience. "You have to be careful in picking the people for whom you provide executive coaching. You want others to clearly understand executive coaching is meant for people who have long runways, as opposed to those who look like they're going off the tracks."

Stu summarized the importance of leadership in today's organizations: "Business leaders who deliver extraordinary performance are those who are able to create a culture where there's a profound commitment to growing their business and their personal leadership effectiveness at one and the same time. Those leaders are exquisitely sensitive to their impact on others and fully committed to bringing out the very best in everyone around them."

Ask the Partners

Q: Do you think your leadership style impacts your company's culture and performance? (Yes, of course you do.) What's the best way you know to get honest and constructive feedback on your way of leading others?

A: Pat has had success applying a model from executive coach and author Marshall Goldsmith: Ask, Listen, Think, Thank, Respond, Change, Involve, Follow up.

For leaders, asking for feedback can be difficult enough. But listening is the true test. You have to be willing to listen to feedback without judging or getting defensive. Responding often means acting to change or modify something for which the feedback is negative. You must be both *trusting* (in your direct control) and *trustworthy* (must be earned over time) in the process and do whatever is necessary to create a safe, no-reprisal environment. In this respect, the CHRO has tone-setting responsibility both personally, for him or herself, and for the organization at large. You need to develop an understanding about how the changes to your style and behaviors will help to bend the culture curve in a positive way.

Goldsmith suggests focusing on just one or two areas for change. He also reminds us that change invariably takes longer than we think, and that the process is difficult. Acknowledging these facts up front can improve success.

chapter eighteen | **Connecting Next Generation Leaders**

Nicola Hain
Founder, The Key Club International (London)

Three years ago, Nicola Hain was one of only 30 senior executives nominated to participate in Ernst & Young's Accelerated Leadership Programme in the UK—and she was the youngest. Despite that accolade, Nicola left E&Y shortly after to found The Key Club International, an innovative approach to creating networks among the next and new generations of business and industry leaders. In 2010, Prime Minister Gordon Brown recognized Nicola as one of the UK's 24 leading women in business. Last year, she was invited to consult with the staff of the Forum of Young Global Leaders, an initiative of the World Economic Forum.

Nicola Hain identified a niche opportunity to build a community that would bring together the next generation of corporate leaders and the new generation of entrepreneur leaders who are shaping the future of business—and she went for it. That was a gutsy move for a young woman who had the chance for a brilliant career at E&Y. In the past 18 months she had achieved remarkable progress toward her goal.

Hard Copy Marketing in the Digital Age

When Nicola set out to market The Key Club International two years ago, she knew she had to aim high. It was "go big or go home." She developed a marketing plan that was both simple and audacious.

"I write very nice letters," Nicola said. "Actual, physical letters with handwritten envelopes. Because nobody gets letters anymore. The whole ethos of The Key Club is building personal relationships. Personal letters mean you've taken the time to reach out to that individual. That seems to have impressed the current generation of leaders."

In fact, Nicola wrote to 700 CEOs, chairmen and presidents to gain their endorsement for The Key Club and request a meeting with them and their senior HR officers. "I wanted to reach out initially to the senior leadership community because I felt that's where the most resonance would be. And it was absolutely true. I got 246 endorsements of support from those 700 letters. The response was absolutely fantastic. So many of them said to me, 'I wish that I'd had this 25 years ago when I was building my career. To think of the contacts that I could have made. That would have been an enormous benefit.' Interestingly enough, several said, 'You should launch a Key Club for our generation.' I said, 'Next phase, next phase.' The letters also enabled me to meet with 76 of them, inviting them to become Founding Mentors for the intergenerational mentoring program that we were launching as a Key community collaboration."

As a result of her marketing efforts, Nicola's list of founding mentors reads like a "Who's Who" of British business and industry. And she recently added Kevin Eyres, former Managing Director, Europe, for LinkedIn as an advisor.

Creating a Network

In a nutshell, Nicola is working to connect the next generation of leaders—those on a clear trajectory to a C-level position—at a point in their careers where it's both easier and more advantageous to make influential connections with their peers, and important to have access to inspiring current generation leaders. Heidi Roizen, the Silicon Valley venture capitalist and former entrepreneur, is the subject of the infamous Harvard Business School case study on leadership networking. That case aptly summed up Nicola's position: "'It's easier to get to know people when they're not famous; then when they do become famous, you already have a relationship with them,' [Roizen said]. Roizen's willingness to invest time in developing relationships with people whom she simply found interesting and smart, as opposed to powerful, paid off repeatedly throughout the years." (Harvard Business School case 9-800-228, "Heidi Roizen," p. 3.) And just to close the loop: After reading the Harvard networking case study about Heidi Roizen, Nicola personally reached out to Heidi to explain The Key Club—and got a ringing endorsement. Heidi pronounced it "totally cool."

"The ability to build influential networks is recognized an essential skill set of C-level leaders, and the importance of leadership networking is incredibly well supported and identified in academic circles," said Nicola. "But there isn't an effective way to put that into practice. It's often something an organization may not have identified as a key development opportunity until too late a stage, when it becomes difficult or even impossible to build the depth and breadth of relationships a C-level executive is expected to have coming into the boardroom."

Nicola described the typical networking wine-and-cheese event from hell that is all too familiar. "Walking into a room where you don't know anybody can fill most people with dread. You're talking to someone and all too soon you get the feeling that they're looking over your shoulder to see who else they could meet—without even knowing if you're someone in a position to help them." Nicola wanted to change that model and make sure that, at least for The Key Club's members, those days are definitely over; everyone in the room is each other's peer.

Research on networks shows that connecting and doing some sort of homework *before* attending an event is absolutely essential for success. "With The Key Club, the connections are made online through our private, peer-to-peer, closed social network." In addition, Nicola pointed out that Sir Martin Sorrell, the highly influential head of the British marketing giant WPP Group, has said that closed, more private networks and communities were going to become more important. He also predicted that people are going to demand closed systems in which they will pay for privacy away from the transparency of today's social networking sites.

"The Key Club's intelligent relationship software—think matchmaking for business introductions—creates best-match teams and introduces teammates online ahead of face-to-face relationship building events. Matches to teammates are based on business and personal interests, as well as the member's preferred industry perspectives."

Online conversations continue through innovative collaborations. As Nicola explained, "We're getting around that whole walking-into-a-room-not-knowing-anybody thing. You're pre-matched to a team. You come together for a bit of friendly competition, which peaks in a challenge event. The Key Club events are money-can't-buy experiences, like cooking along live with a Michelin-starred chef. We had an event with Tom Aikens, the world's youngest-ever, two Michelin-starred chef. Before dinner, Tom, now 41 and a member of The Key Club, shared his experience and challenges he had faced, being thrown on to the world's stage as a global leader in his industry at just 26. These events offer phenomenal ways to share industry and personal experiences, know-how and skills of the people within our membership community."

Nicola has found that philanthropic initiatives are highly effective at uniting people, building relationships and a community around common values. Last year, 46 teams took part in the pilot of The Key Club's Business Friend intergenerational mentoring program. Each of the 46 CEOs, chairmen and presidents collaborated with a member of The Key Club to mentor a young rising star—typically an early 20-something without access to this type of expertise. The rising star's goal is to gain valuable insights and help with getting into an industry or with starting a new business venture or social-entrepreneurship enterprise. "Each project is really a way to build a relationship. And the great thing is that a young rising star gets the benefit of having two mentors, bringing different generational perspectives and experience, advising him or her."

And as Nicola summed it up: "The ethos at The Key Club is to make connections that start conversations that lead to collaborations that build a community." (See illustration, page 169.)

Traditional senior leadership networks usually have some common denominator, most often business school. But that may not continue. Some companies are challenging the value proposition of an MBA. And others, like Lincoln Financial Group, are working with business school faculty on organization-specific programs that offer a better return on their investment.

And the world has changed. "We're now looking at talent and the next generation of leaders coming from much more diverse backgrounds," said Nicola. "It's highly unlikely that they would have had a common connector or an opportunity to meet one another at an earlier stage in their careers. I'm very much hoping that The Key Club will become that common connection. I see it as a platform from which they can meet, build relationships, develop their relationship-building skills and their influence as brand ambassadors for their organizations. The Key Club offers a long-term strategy to build deep relationships, which will pay dividends for the members and their organizations in the future."

Engaging with HR, PR and Marketing

Of course, none of that happens without nominations from The Key Club's member organizations. Nicola doesn't get involved in the selection of The Key Club participants. "Engaging with the HR community has been absolutely essential because they drive and lead the people agenda. Recently, I've also been reaching out to directors in the communications space, like PR and Marketing, to help next generation leaders develop that ambassadorial profile they all have to have."

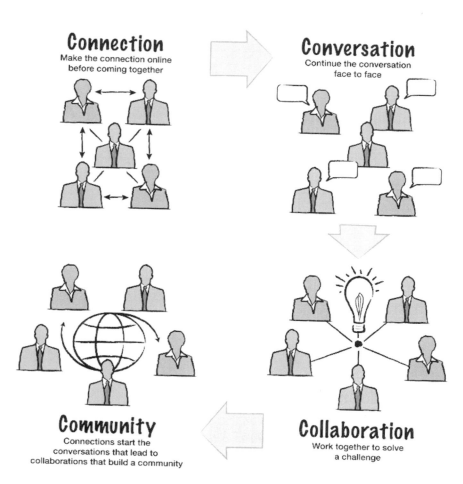

Ask the Partners

Q: The economic downturn has had a disproportionate impact on Millennials—the 18-year-old to 30-something workforce—both here in Europe and worldwide. For example, Spain has reported a 50 percent unemployment rate among workers under 25, and one-third of the youth in Ireland are unemployed. How will this affect their long-term careers? And what steps should employers be taking?

A: There's little doubt that Millennials have lost time and valuable career growth opportunities. In addition to unemployment, people in this group have also suffered from underemployment—working at jobs below their level of education or potential. It will be difficult for them to make up for lost ground.

When the global economy recovers—and it will, ultimately—and baby boomers finally pull the trigger on their delayed retirement, companies will be hiring younger employees in large numbers. These new hires may be lacking critical skills and perhaps some of the social experiences, like working effectively as part of a team, that are important to career success.

Smart companies will address this in their strategic workforce planning, to identify the skills they will need, as well as the most likely skill gaps they will have to address. They'll be prepared to provide accelerated on-the-job training and development to help their new employees catch up as quickly as possible.

chapter nineteen | **Marketing to Employees to Drive Performance**

Doug Newhouse
Partner, Sterling Investment Partners

Doug Newhouse is a managing partner and co-founder of Sterling Investment Partners, based in Westport, Connecticut. Sterling makes private equity investments in middle-market businesses that have strong, sustainable competitive advantages and growth potential. The current portfolio includes Fairway Market, a full-service grocery retailer in the metropolitan New York area, and Excelligence Learning, a leading provider of educational products and programs for children from infancy to age 12. Sterling works with their companies' leadership teams to drive superior financial performance.

When Sterling acquires a company, the partners are betting a substantial amount of money—their investors' as well as their own personal funds—on the future performance of that company. They use strict financial criteria to evaluate potential acquisitions, scrutinizing the company's past performance and growth potential. Although the numbers are paramount, the partners also include some "softer" measures in their evaluation. They're looking for low turnover, open and complete communications and, most important, a strong culture. "Companies that thrive," said Doug, "are the ones that have a set of core values that are communicated on a consistent basis. There's got to be a consistent theme that's delivered. And it has to be understood by all."

After the acquisition, it's all about alignment. Doug is quick to point out that Sterling doesn't micromanage their portfolio companies. They recognize that the company can't be successful without the management team driving that success. But Doug and his partners do have certain expectations, especially around the strategic goals that need to be communicated, that have implications for both HR and Marketing.

Marketing should be partnering with HR to accomplish the HR communications goal.

Compensation is a key driver. "We expect to pay management extremely well if there's superior performance," Doug said. "We set up bonus plans that are tied to hitting mutually agreed targets that enable both managers and employees to make outsize compensation. We also provide generous equity programs that allow employees to own increasingly larger percentages of the company, based on the value we ultimately realize on our investment. Employees have the opportunity to create substantial personal wealth."

But the partners recognize, as every HR person knows, that it takes more than compensation for employees to generate superior results. That's where communications plays a critical role.

An investment banker by training, Doug has never worked in HR or Marketing. But he has some strong opinions about how they should work together. "I think that Marketing should be partnering with HR, working hand in glove. HR has a set of communications goals, but Marketing is the one that can provide the creativity and deliverables to achieve those goals." The kinds of materials to deliver the messages run the gamut from posters to meetings to T-shirts to the company intranet. Some of Sterling's portfolio companies are even developing apps for smartphones, which Doug thinks will become an increasingly popular communications tool.

Doug has a very specific recommendation for the HR/Marketing partnership. "I think you need to treat your employees as a separate market from your customers," Doug said. "And I think you need to communicate to that market with a strategic plan in mind. The more you have an integrated marketing plan to your employee base, the better performance you can drive from those employees."

Brand is a critical part of the message. Not surprisingly, Doug is bullish on the idea of employees as brand ambassadors. "It's very important to inoculate the employees across the firm with what the brand represents and what the brand promises." Doug gives the example of Excelligence Learning, a recent Sterling acquisition. "All the employees there know that they are the best-value provider of pre-K supplies, with the highest level of service and the broadest selection of products. Everybody knows that. And that's a consistent message that they go to market with. People have to know that message. I think that's true in any company that's successful."

Not only do the partners expect consistency of communications in their portfolio companies, but they also practice it themselves. "Within Sterling, everyone here knows the core values we have that we promote to all of our companies. There's tremendous consistency internally, with the message we're delivering whenever we speak to anybody about how we view the world and what's important to us."

Doug Newhouse looks at organizations as an investor, while Jay Spach (see page 116) brings the perspective of an OD practitioner. Although they have very different vantage points, they agree on some critical elements. Both believe that organizations with strong cultures and brands tend to be more successful. Both see the value of employees as brand ambassadors. And they share a conviction that HR and Marketing, working together, can achieve goals that are beyond the capability of either working alone.

Ask the Partners

Q: It's amazing to me the kinds of things, about their companies and work lives, I see people putting out on Facebook, Twitter and other social media. It's clear that people don't understand the risks they're taking. I see it as an employee communications issue. What HR and Marketing policies should companies be thinking about in response to social media?

A: The first step, of course, is to have a policy. The policy should establish clear boundaries for use and the potential consequences. Once a comment is posted, it's out there. You don't want to ban access completely; it's impossible to enforce and only encourages noncompliance. But you do want employees to think before they click.

As obvious as this seems, only a small percentage of companies have social media policies in place. To get started, research other companies' policies and their experience. (See our answer to Jack Mullen's question, page 184, for a link to IBM's policy.) There are guidelines, examples and even templates available online. Social media policies vary widely by organization. Tailor yours to your industry, employee population and brand position. For example, those who have pinned their brand position on transparency and easy access for customers encourage their employees to interact with social media as much as possible. Consider an e-learning module to help employees understand the policy and its importance. But keep it simple. Include pertinent information, but don't get bogged down in detail. The more complicated the policy, the lower the compliance.

Finally, create internal advocates. Focus on the positive by making it easy for employees to represent themselves and the organization, on both company-sponsored social media and employees' own networks. As long as your organization has a clear social media policy that is communicated to employees and is understood, this channel just becomes another tool, like email or the phone.

chapter twenty | **Leveraging Talent as a Competitive Advantage**

Jack Mullen
SVP, Marketing, Shopko

Based in Green Bay, Wisconsin, Shopko is a privately held retailer with 15,000 employees and 143 stores, in small- to medium-sized communities, primarily in the upper Midwest and West. Shopko sells clothing, housewares, furniture, jewelry, along with health and beauty products. All locations include pharmacy and optical department offerings. For FY 2011, Shopko had approximately $2 billion in sales. Jack Mullen has been Senior Vice President, Marketing, for four years. He is responsible for protecting, evolving and communicating the brand across all customer touch points.

When you think of leveraging talent as a competitive advantage, what comes to mind? Top graduates from the best engineering schools, perhaps. A new lawyer who headed the law review. Or maybe a high-flying midcareer hire with a proven track record. You probably *don't* think of sales-floor employees in a discount department store. But that's exactly what Shopko and Marketing SVP Jack Mullen have accomplished.

First, a little background. Shopko refers to its employees, from the CEO to the retail floor, as teammates. "Simply put, we felt the need to break down silos and level barriers and ensure that everyone who worked for Shopko felt like part of the team," Jack said. "We began referring to all our employees as teammates, and now it's second nature."

Jack believes that leveraging the talent in his stores is not only an obvious marketing tool, it's also a significant differentiator from Shopko's competitors that supports the brand in a powerful way. "We can't out-price Walmart, and it's difficult for us to consistently out-design Target. But we can use our teammates as a differentiator in our stores, and we think that keeps our customers coming back to us."

Customer surveys and informal feedback support Jack's position. "Our customers tell us constantly that one of the key reasons they shop us over the competition is our friendly, genuine teammates."

What are store teammates doing that impress customers? Jack explained that it's more about attitude than any specific, discrete behaviors. Teammates are attuned to their customers and skilled at picking up cues on what kind of help they might need. They strive to making shopping at Shopko a friendlier, more personal experience.

What's good for customers also seems to make Shopko a good place to work for teammates. Feedback from teammates and even comments posted on social network forums confirm that they like working at Shopko. Although Jack doesn't have quantitative data to support his thesis, he believes that Shopko's store teammates are more tenured than competitors' employees.

Creating Brand Ambassadors

"We absolutely think that teammates are extensions of our marketing department," said Jack. "Our teammates have to be committed to our mission and understand our strategy to be effective ambassadors." Communications is at the heart of enabling Shopko teammates to be effective brand ambassadors, and the company uses a number of channels.

- All store managers, as well as some store teammates, have access to email and the company's intranet for real-time communication between stores and the general office.

- Shopko develops newsletters, posters and videos (more about one of them later) that are available to all teammates in their store's break room.

- And probably the most important communication system, and an integral part of the Shopko culture, is the daily pre-opening morning huddle. Every morning before the store opens, the manager pulls together the full staff to talk about what's important for that day, like sales and promotional events. Content from the huddle is posted in the break room for late-shift teammates.

In addition, Jack and his team meet quarterly with the district managers, and once or twice a year with store managers. It's two-way communications: He shares the marketing strategy and data on what's working and what's not working; the managers relay what they're hearing from customers and what they need in their markets.

In 2010, it was data from research conducted by Versant Solutions that shaped Shopko's customer acquisition strategy. The study confirmed the importance of teammates as the big difference between Shopko and its competitors. Based on those results, Jack's team made a bold move: They decided to feature teammates in the Christmas season TV spots. "It was very much on brand, and it highlighted a key competitive differentiator. It really made our spots stand out."

To leverage teammate involvement in the campaign beyond those featured in the ads, the marketing department created a video presentation focused on the all-important holiday selling season. Store managers showed the video in their morning huddles; late-shift teammates watched it in their break rooms.

The video focused on the importance of each individual teammate in achieving success in the fourth quarter. The three presenters— CEO, COO and Marketing SVP—split up the key messages:

- CEO W. Paul Jones explained the total strategy and thanked store teammates for their hard work.

- COO Mike Bettiga focused on how important store teammates are in driving the results.

- Marketing SVP Jack Mullen shared the marketing support his group was providing for the upcoming Christmas shopping season.

By way of preparation, each of the three presenters made a list of key points and scripted their messages. But when the camera started rolling, they ditched their scripts and spoke from the heart. "We think that's very much on brand," said Jack. "Our leaders are passionate about the business, and that comes through much stronger when it's not scripted. It's much more powerful if it's genuine and reflects the individual's personality."

Some key facts about the video, beyond its content: First, it was "short and sweet," as Jack described it. The running time was less than four minutes. Second, it was done on a shoestring budget.

Our teammates are extensions of our Marketing department.

Finally, and most important, it was a resounding success. "The message was very positive, supportive and appreciative of teammates' hard work. It resonated well with them," Jack said. "We had a very strong quarter in sales and profits, and we felt that this project contributed to that."

Asked if he plans to do another video for this year's holiday season, Jack replied, "Absolutely. It could well become an annual event. It's simple. It's not rocket science—telling teammates what we need them to do, sharing the strategy with them and thanking them. It's something we want to do more of because we see the obvious benefit of it."

When the British share information with or update others, they use the expression "to put them in the picture." Shopko has done a noteworthy job of putting its teammates in the picture, both literally and figuratively. And created effective brand ambassadors as a result.

Growing in a Tough Economy

Shopko is doing a lot of things right, not just with their store teammates. That success has enabled them to grow in a down economy. In 2011, the company launched a new format, Shopko Hometown. These stores are less than half the size of a regular Shopko, offering about 70 percent of the product line. The stores are planned for rural, generally underserved areas, where people may have to drive half an hour or more to shop in a department or discount store. The company opened ten Shopko Hometown stores last year. Based on positive results, the company developed aggressive plans for further expansion. The company's goal is to become the leading general merchandise retailer focused on serving smaller communities across the country with their Shopko Hometown format.

In early 2012, the company took a major step toward that goal. Shopko announced a merger with Pamida, acquiring 194 stores in 17 states that will be converted to the new Shopko Hometown format during the second half of the year. Along with the stores, Shopko acquired thousands of former Pamida employees, bringing the total number of teammates to 20,000.

Jack explained that this new model is all about engaging with each Hometown market. "It really relies more on the connection with each local community. Every teammate in these stores is a critical part of that store's marketing mix." With thousands of new teammates to train as Shopko brand ambassadors, Jack and his Marketing team have their work cut out for them. But he acknowledged that "we're up to the challenge. This is what we do best. And we know it makes a difference for our customers."

Ask the Partners

Q: One of the things that we're looking to leverage is social media. How have other brands used social media to maximize the impact and reach their employees to serve as brand ambassadors, while minimizing risk and controlling the brand position?

A: In our research, we found lots of experts who advocated employees' use of social media to promote their employer's brand—but not much in the way of actual examples. What we did find was an excellent policy that does exactly what you're looking for: encouraging employees to use social media to speak for the company, but in a responsible way that protects that brand.

Take a look at IBM's "Social Computing Guidelines," available at http://www.ibm.com/blogs/zz/en/guidelines.html. These guidelines, which are regularly reviewed and refreshed, are posted on a public Web site so that everyone—employees, customers, shareholders, suppliers, any interested party—can find out exactly what the policy says. IBM actively encourages employees to make use of social media, and provides appropriate guidelines for employees to follow. Here's a sample:

> IBMers are personally responsible for the content they publish online, whether in a blog, social computing site or any other form of user-generated media. Be mindful that what you publish will be public for a long time—protect your privacy and take care to understand a site's terms of service.

For companies looking to develop their own polices, IBM has provided a comprehensive model. Your company's guidelines should reflect your company's industry, marketplace and, most important, your people.

chapter twenty-one | **Leveraging Talent to Sell Success**

Sam Reese
CEO, Miller Heiman

Miller Heiman is a privately held company that develops and markets sales training and consulting services, and helps their clients improve the efficiency and effectiveness of their sales forces. Sam Reese has been its CEO since 2000. During his tenure, Sam has expanded product offerings, developed a world-class network of sales consultants and grown revenue by more than 200 percent. In the process, he has built a culture that is passionate about achieving results for clients. With the company's expanded product offerings and technology initiatives, Miller Heiman is widely regarded as a thought leader in the process and skills that drive superior sales performance.

Sam Reese has heard all the bad jokes about traveling salesmen, used car salesmen and questionable sales tactics. His single-minded purpose is to bring credibility to sales, to promote the function. "What we think about every day is how we can elevate the role, the status, the credibility and the strategic importance of the sales function. Salespeople in many organizations are not respected. Twenty-somethings coming into the workforce don't want to go into sales. That's one of the reasons we spend time talking to universities and colleges. For us, it's all about saying this is a great profession, it's a strategic profession. And oh, by the way, you have to be smart to do it."

Talent at Miller Heiman

Talent is the key to Miller Heiman's success. Sam believes that an organization must first develop their own game plan as it relates to the way they want to work with prospects and clients. That creates the foundation to bring on board people who can effectively execute the plan. "When you're in the services business, your people really *are* your brand," Sam said. There are about 100 employees on the corporate staff; they're responsible for research, development, logistics, support—anything and everything the field people need to be successful. Across the globe there are about 200 sales consultants and distribution partners; half of them located in the United States and half in the rest of the world.

Miller Heiman has developed a very specific profile of sales talent based on years of data and research. "We have an assessment that we put people through. We don't leave it to chance; our talent assessment maps to the behaviors and thinking styles of our top performers. We're looking for people who have the same behaviors as our top performers. We also have a rigorous interview process that goes with the assessment." In particular, Miller Heiman is looking for people who know selling, have experience running large sales organizations and understand how customers make decisions. In addition to practical experience, they're looking for people with an entrepreneurial mindset who are also team players. "That combination sounds unusual, but that's what we look for," explained Sam.

For example, take the position of sales consultant. At Miller Heiman, these are the field people who work directly with clients to sell and deliver training programs and consulting services. The headquarters support team is focused on making it easier for them, serving as a responsive information source for them. "We give them leads that match their sweet spots and the knowledge to help them become experts in certain industries," said Sam. "White papers, webinars, whatever they need. Our job is to keep our sales consultants powered up." In addition, Miller Heiman supports their sales channel with a network of sales vice presidents who have the job of assisting their sales consultants in the areas of business development and account management.

The talent profile for sales consultants includes a very specific background. "All of our sales consultants have to have experience as sales VPs or directors at large companies. We want people out there who have run sales organizations and can look across the table at other sales VPs and say, 'Yes, I know what you're going through.'"

Miller Heiman takes a somewhat unorthodox approach to career development. "We're really big believers in letting people chart their own career paths and find opportunities that help the business," Sam explained. For sales consultants, that could mean expanding into new industries or developing new vertical markets. That entrepreneurial spirit isn't limited to sales consultants in the field. For the support team at headquarters, it means filling a niche that that will improve customer satisfaction. "We've got several people in the organization in jobs that I couldn't have written down five years ago, jobs we didn't even have descriptions for."

Sam cited the example of an executive who identified the need for a client engagement manager. She made the case that in their largest engagements, the field team needed a specialist focused on customization and project planning. "She successfully sold the idea internally because it connected with what customers wanted," Sam said.

> When you're in the services business, your people really *are* your brand.

The company's approaches to talent and career development are clearly successful. Miller Heiman people stay. "We have people who have worked at our company for a long time. We don't have much turnover," Sam said. An even more impressive statistic: The majority of the company's sales consultants are former Miller Heiman clients. "I look at that as a true success metric," explained Sam. "And I use that as a good benchmark for our people internally. They have to continue to show who the Miller Heiman brand is, because the people they're calling on may want to work with us one day."

Selling Sales

For Miller Heiman, selling is not about slick talk or manipulating customers. "You can't manipulate people. It's not honest, and it just doesn't work. Our philosophy, everything we do is about nonmanipulative selling. People are smart and they'll make their own decisions." Rather, successful selling is all about customers—communicating with them, understanding what they need and determining if there's a fit between what you can do and what their problems are. Or as Sam succinctly put it, "What the customer is trying to fix, accomplish or avoid."

Sam's company is in the business of selling sales. "We are on stage in every interaction we have. We've got to be good every time," said Sam. "What we want our customers to say is, 'We want our people to sell the way you sell.' And we say, 'Great!' We are relentless on using our own stuff. That's an important part of our success."

Miller Heiman works mostly with large corporations, but they also offer a number of sales development workshops that are open to the public; the schedules are posted on the Web site. These generic programs are geared to the sales organizations of small- and medium-sized businesses. The bulk of Miller Heiman's work is with corporate sales organizations. Miller Heiman's ideal client is a large B2B organization dealing with complex sales: big ticket items, multiple decision makers and highly competitive. Miller Heiman gains an understanding of the client's unique challenges and then tailors the solution to the individual client's needs. The solution gives the customer a common sales vocabulary and an execution framework that delivers results quickly and drives sustainable performance into the future.

Sam's Blog

Just as Miller Heiman employees have identified new positions in response to customers' needs, Sam started writing his CEO blog for the same reason. (To read Sam's blog, go to http://www.millerheiman.com/blog/sam-reese/) After Sam's presentations at customer events, participants asked if he could share his observations on a more frequent, less formal basis. "I called a few customers, and they started telling me about issues that were troubling them. So I started blogging when I came across something interesting. And the reaction has been pretty amazing," said Sam. "It's been a nice way for me to get more connected to the most senior leaders at our client companies. I can't touch everybody, but now we have this common point. And when I meet with customers, they often refer to my latest blog."

Sam's blog has become an effective tool for product development and updates. "We get a lot of feedback from our clients on the issues they're having. So I'll write about the topic and then realize that we hadn't made the connection, that this was a subject we needed to include in our solutions." But he doesn't use his blog to sell. "I never talk about our products and services, and I never make a sales pitch. Our philosophy is all about nonmanipulative selling. I talk about provocative points that I find interesting, but I don't tie anything to our products. People will stop reading it if it's all about buying a product."

Putting It Together

The secrets to Sam's and Miller Heiman's success are not so secret. A lot of the credit goes to Sam's leadership style. First, everyone understands the purpose of the organization. "For us, the purpose of making sales people credible is what galvanizes us. We're trying to make sure they have real skills and can sustain them. That's what it's all about." Second, Sam and his leadership team are "very big on a core set of principles that revolve around respect for the individual and flexibility. We are believers that work is something we've all got to do, and we all want to be successful at it. We're all going to be really focused. But we know people have lives outside the office, and so we provide a lot of flexibility to our people. There's no issue if somebody has to take a family member to the doctor or wants to go to their daughter's soccer game. At Miller Heiman, it's all about the results you deliver."

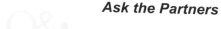

Ask the Partners

Q: Over the last decade, how have employees changed their views around their company and their careers, and I'd say specifically as it relates to job security and loyalty?

A: The contract between employer and employee has been reset. Employer loyalty to employee has eroded steadily and consistently for 20 years. We know that the sense of job security is gone for employees; likewise, many employers have lost their sense of economic security. In this environment, younger employees, in particular, are likely to feel that they're trying to build their careers on sand.

The new challenge is creating loyalty and alignment in a "free agency" atmosphere. Begin by ensuring that all employees understand how their roles link to the organization's goals, and how their behavior in that role supports achieving those goals. That understanding can create a strong connection and alignment that can ultimately lead to loyalty. Smart companies also provide the right work environment, development opportunities and managers who can coach and develop their people. If the employee stays, the company has the benefit of a skilled, motivated worker. Employees who opt to move to other companies leave with a strong résumé and a positive experience.

chapter twenty-two | **Leading the Digital Transformation**

Adrian Butler
CHRO, Cengage Learning

Cengage Learning is a leading provider of innovative teaching, learning and research solutions for the academic, professional and library markets worldwide. Among the company's brands are Brooks/Cole, Delmar, Course Technology, Gale, National Geographic Learning, South-Western and Wadsworth. Based in Stamford, Connecticut, Cengage Learning has 5,500 employees in 20 countries. Adrian Butler is Executive Vice President of Human Resources, responsible for ensuring that the company's global HR strategies are aligned with the overall business goals. He also sits on the seven-member Executive Committee.

Cengage Learning is in the midst of a major transformation: The educational publishing market is moving from print to digital. Following in the footsteps of other industries—music, movies and mainstream publishing—educational publishing is probably the last of the industries of this scale to go digital. And the speed of the transformation is accelerating.

"The business model is changing," said Adrian. "The particular product that we have become very adept and very successful at producing is the textbook. The textbook is not going to go away in the short term, but today's students and instructors are relying less on textbooks. They are already buying hybrid products, a mixture of traditional textbooks and electronic. Increasingly, they're looking for pure digital solutions and tools."

Practically everything about the way Cengage Learning does business, from product development to marketing, is changing. In the print world, content was king. Textbook authors had the luxury of two or three years to develop a product that would have a shelf life of several years. Now, time to market is an equally critical factor. Development has been compressed to a matter of months, with the expectation of frequent updates and revisions. Once a semester is the new norm, and several Cengage Learning programs include real-time updates, with new content continuously streamed in. The table below summarizes some of the key differences between the past publishing model and the present.

	Old School	Digital World
Customer	Individual professors	Students, faculties, institutions
End user	The student	The student
Product offering	Textbooks	Subscriptions or license fees for books— or even specific chapters
Point of sale	College bookstore	Online
Success factor	The best content	Getting to market first, at the right price point
Development cycle	2 to 3 years	2 to 3 months
Revision cycle	3 to 4 years	By semester; or even real time, with streamed content
Culture	Conservative, risk averse	Innovative, risk taking
Key talent	Textbook authors	Programmers, experienced online learning program developers, subject matter experts
Measures of engagement	None – too difficult or expensive	Counting clicks, recorded time within programs and, ultimately, improved student outcomes

For the time being, however, Cengage Learning is operating in a "both/and" world. "If we just continue to do what we did, we'll fail.

And if we just threw out all our textbooks tomorrow, we'd fail. We need to transform the business in a measured and responsible way, while protecting the revenue stream for a product that may one day become nearly obsolete."

The transformation has triggered Adrian to focus on two key areas. First, it required him to redefine what *talent* means for Cengage Learning and actively jump-start some cultural changes. Second, the transformation inspired him to focus on the importance of the brand and to reach out to Marketing.

New Talent for a New Culture

Adrian recognizes that the expertise required for building effective digital learning programs is different from the skills for publishing traditional textbooks. The content may be similar, but the delivery mechanism is altogether different. Adrian is approaching his talent needs with a combination of build and buy.

On the build side, the company is offering training for current employees on the new skills required in the digital world and to promote innovation. "There's always an argument whether you can train people to be creative," Adrian said. [See his question for Pat and Will, page 201.] "Nevertheless, we work hard at actually helping people understand that part of their job is to think forward."

Cengage Learning is literally putting money on its people to spark innovation and challenge the risk-averse culture. "In the technology world, you have to take some bets. We actually give our business people R&D dollars to try some things. Not everything is going to fly;

you have to take some chances. If people feel it's an environment where they can make mistakes, they're going to be more creative," Adrian said.

On the buy side, bringing in new talent—employees with technology skills and more innovative mindsets—facilitates product development and helps transform the culture. "When you take people who have great knowledge of the industry and content but haven't got the technology skills, and you bring in the technology skills and you get them to talking, working in a collaborative way, you have something there."

Bringing in talent with the required technology background and experience called for new recruiting strategies in new fields. The company has produced a series of videos that feature Cengage Learning employees marketing the company to potential employees. [To watch, go to http://www.cengage.com/careers/employee-videos/]

Marketing is a key partner for HR.

Somewhat reluctantly, Adrian admitted that some current employees won't make the trip, and that you have to make tough decisions on people who might stall innovation and jeopardize progress. In a rapidly changing business world, old business models are no longer effective. To be successful in the long term, Adrian believes that the appropriate talent management strategy is a combination of retooling, retraining and replacing your workforce.

Branding Cengage Learning, Inside and Out

Adrian pointed out that CHROs typically work very hard to align themselves with Finance, saying that the two functions should "challenge each other, but work together." In Adrian's opinion, that collaboration is necessary but not sufficient on its own. "Marketing is also a key partner for HR," he said.

"If HR just concentrates its attention on aligning itself and working hand-in-hand with Finance, that reinforces the service function, back-office operation, cost-control mindset; it's very internally focused. Working with Marketing—that's all about selling the company and helping the company in a forward-thinking way. And with an external focus. It's important you do both. I'm not suggesting you do one or the other."

That forward thinking and external focus led Adrian to consider the Cengage Learning brand. Although the company has a long history with several well-known brands, like Gale in the library reference market, the name Cengage Learning is relatively new. Short for "center of engagement," it was coined in 2007, when the Thomson Corporation sold what was then Thomson Learning to a group of investors. Under Thomson, the company was a collection of acquisitions. Each of the educational publishing companies had different brands and different cultures. Over the past three or four years, Cengage Learning has successfully integrated those companies.

But integration was just the first step. "We have some work to do in terms of building the Cengage Learning brand identity externally, which will help customers. But it will also help our employees. HR can do a great deal, especially in partnership with Marketing, to articulate our identity, and help us promote it both within the company and without. If we can brand ourselves better, we can help our employees articulate the company better externally. The culture in the organization is not to blow our own trumpet, which makes it a nice environment in which to work. But I think at times we could be a little bit more aggressive and proactive in this because it's a great marketing tool to get our message out there."

Looking Ahead

As difficult as the transformation is, it offers Cengage Learning some real advantages. It puts the company in closer contact with students. With online offerings, the student is often the customer as well as the end user. That makes it easier for Cengage Learning to market directly to students. As Adrian explained, "The secret sauce to our business is student engagement. If we can get fully engaged students who really are actively participating in an educational program, not only will they achieve success, but they'll also keep coming back for more."

Digital products also facilitate an easy, meaningful metric. "The great thing about technology is that you can measure engagement," said Adrian. "You don't know how many times a person's looked at their textbook. You don't even know if they've opened the front cover. But you can count clicks. And institutions are very interested in that data because that gives them a sense as to how strong the product is to future students."

So Cengage Learning looks forward to a future that offers both challenges and promise. Along with managing the transformation, Adrian and his team will continue to do the core work of HR that has made them successful:

- Maintaining a good infrastructure and systems to handle transactional work, which facilitates

- Focusing on being more strategic in the way they support the business and

- Aligning everything they do in support of the business goals and

- Creating an environment with motivated, engaged, high-performing people in the right jobs at the right time, which supports

- Developing and retaining the best talent.

As Adrian concluded, and as every HR person knows, "Ultimately, our success as a function is determined to a large extent by how well we counsel and advise, and to some extent prod and poke, our line managers into doing the right things, first by the business and then by the people."

Ask the Partners

Q: In a business transformation situation like our own, and all businesses are transforming to some extent, can you teach creativity? Can you teach innovation? Or is it completely innate? There are a lot of organizations out there that have run innovation programs in some shape or form. I haven't read enough to know how successful you can truly be. To what extent can you be successful in developing innovation with your existing workforce?

A: There are definitely steps you can take to foster innovation in your workforce. We suggest a two-pronged approach. The first is around expectations. Set the expectation that all employees have a creative/innovative bent—because they do!—and that you want them to find it and use it in their work. Build understanding of the desired behaviors by seeking out examples of individual and team innovation. Communicate these examples across the organization and watch what will surface. Engage the leadership team; their words and actions should reinforce that innovation is a valued behavior.

Second, and probably more important, is a culture audit. Are you enabling the growth/development of a culture that *demands* creativity and encourages risk taking and moving away from the status quo? Do you reward and recognize creativity and innovation and encourage (and fund) follow-through to bring ideas to fruition? Or are you process-oriented and focused on increasing the efficiency of what you currently or typically do? For many employees, creativity is outside their comfort zone. So they will opt for what they know will be appreciated, respected and usually rewarded. Make sure that your policies and practices are focused on what the company needs.

chapter twenty-three | **Planning to Collaborate**

David Ballard
*Assistant Executive Director, Marketing and Business Development,
American Psychological Association*

David Ballard designs and directs efforts related to health and well-being in the workplace. In that capacity, he spearheads APA's Psychologically Healthy Workplace Program designed to help employers create a workplace culture that promotes both employee well-being and organizational performance. David oversees a Web site, an e-newsletter, a blog and podcasts, as well as face-to-face and virtual learning events and a robust social media presence. The organization also bestows APA's Psychologically Healthy Workplace Awards. David has experience in management, marketing and consumer research. He serves on several boards, including The Health Project's C. Everett Koop National Health Awards, the Health Enhancement Research Organization and the Mayo Clinic Center for Social Media Advisory Board. A frequently requested speaker, David regularly addresses professional audiences throughout the United States and Canada. He earned his PsyD in clinical psychology and MBA in health and medical services administration from Widener University.

With a background in Psychology and Marketing, and lots of experience working with HR professionals around North America, David Ballard seemed a natural to offer advice on how HR and Marketing heads could initiate a collaboration. For organizations where the two functions aren't currently working together, David's suggestions could provide just the stimulus.

Look for the mutual benefit. An effective collaboration has to benefit both parties; otherwise, it's going to feel like one department is stepping on the other's toes. "It's not about taking over a part of what one group does; it's about finding ways that both can achieve better results," said David. "Make sure you're speaking the language of the other group and focusing on things that are actually important to them. [Authors' note: See Jay Spach's Brand Continuum, page 118, for a starting point to explore mutual benefits.]

Make the business case. In addition to the advantages for HR and Marketing, show the connection between the collaboration and achieving the organization's overarching goals. Increasing the engagement of customer-facing employees, for example, could have a direct impact on customer satisfaction.

Understand what each does. David made the point that people's perceptions about what certain departments do can vary. A lot of people think Marketing just focuses on advertising. In reality, Marketing is doing everything from assessing needs to competitive research to product positioning before they even begin to craft the advertising messages. Outside of HR, a lot of people tend to think HR is just about employee benefits. They don't think about all the other areas—recruiting, development, leadership training, recognition—where HR has a direct bearing on the performance of the company. Each side should understand the skills they want to engage from the other discipline, and be prepared to explain the skills they bring to the partnership.

Find a champion. "When you're pitching a collaboration, especially one that may not necessarily be a natural one in a particular organization, it's crucial to find a champion. Find one person in that other department that you can connect with, someone who can champion the effort from within their own team."

Start small. Starting with a pilot or other small project is much less threatening than immediately trying to overhaul the relationship between HR and Marketing. "Once you've demonstrated some success, with those small wins under your belt, you can make the case for expanding the collaboration to other efforts."

The Psychologically Healthy Workplace*

One of the areas that could benefit from a joint HR/Marketing collaboration is the psychologically healthy workplace. That's the term David uses to describe a systemic approach that both fosters employee well-being and enhances the performance and productivity of the organization. "It balances employee and organizational outcomes to get the best results possible for all parties involved," said David. "Historically, workplace programs and policies have been viewed as one or the other. Either they're focused on the benefit to the employee, which some employers simply see as a cost, or they are designed to squeeze as much productivity as possible out of the workforce, which can come at the expense of employee health.

* For more on creating a healthy, high-performing organization, see APA's Psychologically Healthy Workplace Program Web site at http://www.phwa.org.

"In the past, well-being and performance were two separate paths. What we've come to realize is they're inextricably linked. When employees thrive, you get better organizational outcomes. And an organization that's more successful can also promote employee well-being."

David said that there's no single way to create a psychologically healthy workplace. "A lot of the success of these programs depends on how well an organization tailors its efforts to meet the needs of the workforce and the organization itself. The kinds of things employers are doing tend to fall into five categories, all held together by effective communications practices."

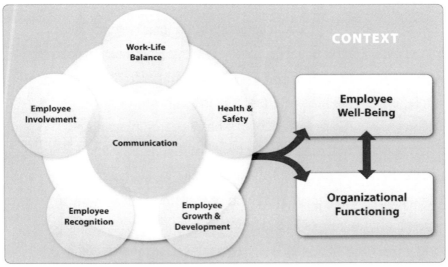

© American Psychological Association. Reprinted with permission.

And communication is critical. David said, "I often talk about communications being the hub of the wheel. You have all these practices that rotate around the outside, and the glue that holds them together is communications. Without effective two-way

communications, it's very difficult to achieve the results you want."
Most HR people have experience in the program areas, but
Marketing could clearly play a role in communications. Their
creativity in crafting messages and their expertise in two-way
communications in the marketplace could be real assets. Marketers
also tend to have more experience in using social media. "The use
of social media to communicate is here to stay. Increasingly,
employers will have to find effective ways to use these tools in ways
that employees are open to," said David.

Marketing's creativity in crafting messages could be a real asset.

Designed, implemented and communicated effectively,
psychologically healthy workplace practices yield measurable
benefits for employees. "Employees experience better physical and
mental health. They report higher levels of job satisfaction. They're
more motivated at work. They feel more committed to the
organization. They say the climate of the organization is more
positive. And they're better able to handle the stress that they face
on a day-to-day basis. So it has a lot of benefits for the employees,"
David said.

And it's not just employees who benefit. "There's a strong business
case for creating a healthy workplace. Organizations see reductions
in absenteeism. They see less turnover; their accident and injury
rates go down. It can reduce health care costs, or slow the rate of

increase. Organizations also see higher levels of performance and productivity. Their product and service quality goes up, their customer service and satisfaction ratings improve. And they're able to recruit and retain the very best workers. In today's business environment, where human capital is the competitive advantage, they're able to attract and keep the best and the brightest."

David acknowledged that even good companies had to make some difficult decisions during the recession. "In a survey the APA conducted, two-thirds of employees reported that their employers had made cuts, like laying off staff, freezing wages or scaling back benefits. Interestingly, at the time this was happening, we were seeing surveys that showed *higher* levels of employee satisfaction and engagement."

David shared two hypotheses to explain the apparent contradiction. "In organizations that were handling it well, employees were banding together to help each other and their company make it through the tough times. These companies fostered loyalty, engagement and trust. In organizations that didn't handle it as well, employees hunkered down, saying 'At least I still have a job and I'm certainly not going to make waves.' But beneath that facade they were unhappy, distrustful and waiting for the other shoe to drop. As the economy starts to turn around, those employees are beginning to look for a better work environment."

Ask the Partners

Q: How can small- and medium-sized companies effectively promote and create healthy and productive work environments? How can these organizations make strides in their communication efforts when they may not have a whole marketing department to look to? So that's my question: How do we work with the small employer so that they can benefit from these approaches as well?

A: Use size to your advantage. What small organizations lack in resources, they more than compensate for in agility. And small employers often have the benefit of knowing everyone in their organizations. So, make it personal! Lead by example. Get creative. For example, sponsor a contest for a free gym membership.

Explore turnkey opportunities. Invite the local YMCA or community center to present their offerings at a brown-bag lunch. Hospitals often have community outreach staff members who speak with groups about fitness, smoking cessation or weight-management programs. Publicize flu shots and free health screenings when offered by neighborhood drug stores

To facilitate employee development, look for online learning programs that you can make available to a wide employee audience for a modest licensing fee.

Do a policy audit. Look at your policies and practices, both formal and informal. Do they encourage people to renew and refresh? For example, do people make time for family, friends and community? Does the organization respect people's not-at-work time? Small, targeted efforts can have big payoffs in these environments.

chapter twenty-four | **Summing it Up**

George Graham
Graham Consulting, Ltd.

George Graham holds a Ph.D. from Marquette University, and he was a Danforth Fellow at the University of Chicago. He began his career as a teacher in clinical counseling in several university settings; George later migrated to the field of industrial/ organizational psychology. From the mid-1970s through the early '90s, he held a number of senior positions at the First Wisconsin National Bank and its successors. George has served and continues to serve on the boards of a number of local nonprofit organizations. He currently maintains a consulting practice in the Milwaukee area serving clients seeking to resolve Human Resources and Organizational Development issues.

With the benefit of a six-decade long career, George Graham has had the opportunity to distill his cogent observations about organizations and people.

Organizations

George defines an organization as "a group of people with a common purpose; both elements can be measured." And as simple and straightforward as that definition seems, George has observed that many organizations don't satisfy it. Lack of focus, internal politics and inconsistency lead to breakdowns in the efficiency and effectiveness of the organization. All organizations have a distinct

211

function. A business is a particular kind of organization, one that provides products or services to meet a specific need. "The business of business is to be needed and to serve others. In other words, it should be doing something for the culture or it's not going to last," George said.

"An enduring company endures because of its reputation." For George, Marketing is really about creating and expanding a company's reputation. Good reputations are built on honesty, product quality and distinctive service. Increasingly, companies' reputations now also depend on their decisions in times of crisis. It takes time and consistency to establish a reputation that can be destroyed in a matter of days.

"Organizations, like people, have personalities. Each has its own personality, reflecting its leadership style and cultural heritage," George said. Apple and IBM are both large, high-tech companies, but they have very different personalities. "Talented people can be successful in one organization and fail to achieve their potential in another." In cases of personality mismatches, the best option, for both the individual and the company, is to move on. George offers the example of sports teams, where a mediocre player on one team moves to another and shows marked improvement.

"The concept of line and staff just has to go." George reserved his most pointed comments for the line-and-staff organizational model, which he sees as hopelessly outdated. Based on the structure of the Roman army, it worked for Julius Caesar's military campaigns. It worked for the cathedral builders in the late Middle Ages. And George believes that it was still reasonably effective up to the early

20th century. But it doesn't work for today's complex organizations that rely on highly specialized and technically skilled functions. Traditional "staff" functions are so critical to the success of an organization that the old distinction is irrelevant. "Information technology is just as important as manufacturing or sales. Without state-of-the-art IT, today's businesses simply couldn't function," said George. "And that's true for all the other 'staff' functions like Legal and Accounting."

People

If an organization is a group of people with a common purpose, then it's the leader's responsibility to ensure that everyone is aligned with that common purpose. "To be effective, employees must have a keen sense of their place in the organization, and how their work relates to the purpose," George said.

Marketing is about creating and expanding a company's reputation.

"Outstanding leaders don't have subordinates." In place of subordinates they have partners working with them to achieve a shared goal. And that's the way a true leader treats the people in his or her organization. As human beings, each of us has a deep need to be recognized for who we are and what we can and want to do. "I remind leaders that these so-called 'subordinates' have the same feelings and motivation that they do. All of us are motivated by positive answers to the questions, 'Is this a good place for me? Will I be recognized for what I can do?'

"Good leaders understand that the more they talk, the less they learn. They already know what they know; they need to know what their associates know and think." As a psychologist, businessman and consultant, George listens carefully. "In diagnostic work, when I encounter a person who has all the answers, I know that's an indication that they're not ready for change. In business, those who do the most talking are often the least secure." Good managers listen to their people, which enables them to be more effective coaches, mentors and role models.

Like virtually everyone else we interviewed for this book, George shared his thoughts on talent. His advice: "Promote those who do the best job of developing others. As people move up in responsibility, their work demands less in the way of technical expertise and more interpersonal and leadership skills," said George. "And the greatest of these skills is the ability to identify potential in others and provide for their development. Leadership itself is a matter of relationship, where an associate in the enterprise has the deep feeling that 'because of my boss, this is the place where I can be and do my best.'"

Ask the Partners

Q: As leaders of organizations, how do you create an environment where associates and employees make the statement, "This is the company where I can do my best"?

A: We create these work environments through talent vigilance. That means being obsessed with getting, developing and promoting the best possible talent. Create an open marketplace within the organization and make sure successful, high-performing, talented people are seen throughout the organization. Recognize their accomplishments and reward them in a meaningful and effective way—with more opportunity, more responsibility, proper resources, promotions as well as financial rewards.

chapter twenty-five | **Making Effective Videos**

Greg Cooke
Director of Photography with credits on "60 Minutes" and "CBS Reports"

Greg Cooke is a professional Director of Photography based in Los Angeles. He has worked extensively in broadcast television, taping hundreds of interviews for network news and shows like "60 Minutes." Greg also works with corporate clients, creating videos for CEOs and other senior leaders to communicate with their employees.

In the age of YouTube, video is part of virtually every company's employee communications strategy. Video can be a powerful and effective way for leaders to communicate with employees—or it can be a disaster. The difference between the two comes down to careful planning and execution. Greg Cooke provided some advice and trade secrets to producing effective, professional quality videos.

First, a little background. Modern video equipment is much smaller than earlier models. When Greg does on-site corporate shoots, all the equipment he needs fits neatly into a couple of cases not much bigger than gym bags. All of Greg's equipment is battery operated, eliminating the need for heavy cables. Images and voices are recorded on solid state cards, professional versions of the ones used in consumer cameras. Today's cameras start and stop instantly, and they can operate at much lower lighting levels, reducing the need for multiple light stands.

As a result, the whole process today is much more low key than in the past. "We can walk into somebody's office, sit down, conduct an interview, put our stuff back in the cases and walk out," Greg said. "Many times people in the same part of the building never knew we were there." Any truly professional crew, Greg advises, should be just as unobtrusive.

Compact equipment and the low-key process also works to the advantage of Greg's corporate clients. "For the corporate leader, this setup is much more comfortable. It's much less daunting to just sit down and have a conversation, almost in available light or the normal lighting level of the room."

For people new to video, Greg's advice is to study professional interviews on television. The first thing to notice is that the interview subject is not looking directly at the camera. As humans, we're programmed to make eye contact with a person, not a camera lens. "Nobody wants to look directly at the camera. A camera doesn't have an actual personality to it," Greg pointed out. "The people are generally looking slightly off to the side of the lens, one way or the other. That's the technique used in broadcasting today. The conversational interview where the person is not looking directly into the lens is the accepted norm."

So where is the person looking? He or she is making eye contact with an interviewer—who may or may not ever be heard or seen on camera. In television, that person could be the producer or documentary narrator. In corporate videos, it's often the head of communications—or it could be you, if you're producing a video for one of your projects.

Looking directly at a camera—without being self-conscious—is a skill that takes years to develop. Network anchors have acquired that skill, and they do it effortlessly. Others are less successful at pulling it off. "If you're looking directly into the lens, it seems more like a pitchman trying to sell something than a CEO delivering a message in an honest, engaging way," Greg commented.

What about teleprompters? In fact, here's the very first thing Greg said in his interview, before the opening question was even posed: "Don't use a teleprompter; throw the teleprompter away!" Teleprompters may have their place—for speeches at a political convention, say—but not in corporate videos.

To put Greg's other suggestions in context, assume for the moment that you're the head of HR for your company. You've been working with your Marketing counterpart on employer branding, and part of your communications rollout includes a video of the CEO.

Planning Ahead

If you don't have in-house video capability, you'll need to engage a professional crew. Poll colleagues for recommendations. Ask potential suppliers for references. Most important, ask to see samples of their corporate interviews. Does the interview look like the ones you see on television? Does the speaker look relaxed? Does he or she come across as believable? Choose professionals that have demonstrated that they can create the kind of video you need.

Content is critical. What do you want the CEO to say? Greg is quick to point out that conversations are not the same as speeches. "As human beings, we speak differently when we talk than when we type words," Greg said. "When someone types up a speech, they're looking at things like correct grammar and punctuation. They're sort of reading it in their mind, but they're not actually speaking the words. As soon as people start to speak those printed words, it *sounds* like printed words. It sounds like a setup."

Rather than a script, Greg advises preparing a set of talking points that you and the CEO agree should be covered in the video. Keep in mind that it's not a speech, it's a conversation. You can then develop a series of questions—or you may need only a few prompts—that will guide the conversation.

You, or even the CEO, may want to do a dry run of the interview. That's fine, says Greg, but he offers a note of caution from one of his colleagues at "60 Minutes": "As Mike Wallace would often say, 'Don't lose it in rehearsal.' Just come relaxed. Nobody knows the material better than the corporate leader. They know everything."

When setting up the shoot on the CEO's calendar, be sure to allow enough time. You don't want the executive to feel rushed or pressured by the next meeting. Greg suggests that you allow at least an hour for a video planned to run five to ten minutes.

Finally, there's wardrobe. Everyone knows to avoid stripes and strong patterns that can create distracting patterns on camera. Greg advises that the CEO should dress as if he or she were having a one-on-one conversation with an employee. If the company's dress policy is business casual, that's how the CEO should dress. If business suits are the norm, the CEO should dress accordingly.

The Video Shoot

A good professional video crew can make almost any space work. They can adapt to lighting conditions and other features of the room and create a picture that's pleasing for the viewer to look at. Greg prefers to work in conference rooms. "Photographically, you want to have a sense of depth behind the person. So you never set anybody up against a wall. You never set a subject up against a bookcase, where viewers could be distracted by trying to read the titles. In a conference room, we'll go to the far end and shoot down toward the other end, to give us the maximum distance. It makes the background appear softer in focus and fuzzy, which leads the viewer to focus in on the sharp detail of the person's face."

Conversations are not the same as speeches.

And speaking of the person's face, Greg typically works with a makeup artist. Although he acknowledges that makeup is not necessary, he aims to make his subjects look their best and eliminate shiny spots on the face (or head!) that could reflect. But too much makeup is worse than none at all. Women will often have a definite preference, either to do their own makeup or to use the services of a professional.

Seating is an important part of the setup. "I would never put anybody directly behind a desk or table, facing straight at me. They might sit sideways to a table and put one elbow on the table. But they're open face, looking my direction; they're not staring across the table at the camera."

Greg avoids chairs that swivel or rock, as well as leather chairs that can squeak. He prefers straight-back chairs that encourage their occupants to sit upright. Not only will they look better on camera, but they're also more likely to speak clearly and "e-nun-ci-ate" their words.

If you're the off-camera interviewer, it's your job to ask the questions that will elicit the talking points. Remember that it's a conversation, not a prepared speech. The CEO will respond using his or her own words—and that's exactly what you want.

Greg cautions about a common mistake that interviewers make. "The interviewer will say, 'Tell me about such and such.' And the CEO responds. Then the interviewer will say something like, 'That was great. But can you do it again, this time starting with the second part of your answer?'" The interviewer is trying to cut and paste the conversation, like editing a document. "When people speak," Greg says, "they don't consciously recall all of the words precisely in the order they said them." It's disconcerting to the interview subject and could throw them off for the remainder of the interview.

Rather than trying to "edit" on the spot, Greg suggests continuing with the interview, moving on to the next question, then circling back. "You have to gently carry on the conversation and guide the CEO back to the points you want to cover, and the editing will take care of the rest."

The Magic of Editing

It's the editor's job to weave together pieces of the conversation to make the final video, where it looks as though your CEO "simply sat down and spoke to somebody sitting very near the lens, talking openly, hitting all of the talking points," Greg said. "The interview process could have gone on for 45 minutes or so. Then out of that, we will glean the talking points and connect them together in the edit in such a way that it's very transparent. In the edit, we bring the thought or the story line complete, with a beginning, middle and end."

In closing, Greg had some final words of wisdom. "The thing is just not to be too uptight about the process. The key word is relax. Everything's going to be just fine."

When the Going Gets Tough:
Advice from a Seasoned Interviewer

During his 40-year career working with both CBS News and ABC News, Morton Dean conducted literally thousands of interviews. He has worked on executive interviews with both Will Ruch and Greg Cooke. Morton is currently a partner at a corporate and executive communications firm, coaching senior executives on how to handle interviews.

The interview sessions Greg described take place under controlled conditions, and there's always the opportunity for another take if the first is less than satisfactory. But executives also face tougher interview situations. Think about the Q&A session at a CEO's Town Hall meeting where employees are likely to ask difficult or sensitive questions. It's happening live and there are no do-overs. Morton Dean, who coaches executives on how to handle these and other tough questions, offered some time-tested advice.

"The first step is convincing the executive it's not worth the risk to go into an interview unprepared. Unfortunately, too many executives don't realize the importance of this until after they've been scorched by a poor performance and are desperate not to let that happen again.

"The three key steps are preparation, preparation, preparation. It's an absolute necessity." With his experience as a long-time news correspondent and with some background on the company, Morton can usually anticipate, with pretty good accuracy, what the questions will be. That enables him to coach executives on how to handle not only the obvious, expected questions, but also the unexpected "gotcha" questions.

Morton also offered a suggestion about a good habit he recommends to his clients. "Here's how I advise my executive clients to make sure they're always prepared: 'Before you leave for work in the morning, think about the toughest question an employee or a journalist could ask you that day, and have your answer before you walk out the door.'"

Executive coach Morton Dean can be reached at mortonndean@aol.com

Ask the Partners

Q: Will Ruch and I have done hundreds of executive video interviews together over the years. I would like to ask him for the one recommendation he would make to the videographer ("video shooter" in the profession) and interviewer to make a great video with an executive.

A: The videographer and the interviewer must be a team. It's critical for the executive to feel comfortable in the conversation. While this may seem obvious, the more harmonious the production twosome is, the more relaxed the executive will appear and the better the interview will be. It's also important to keep it short, nothing more than an hour—aim for half an hour if possible. Executives never complain about getting time back on their calendars.

Afterword

Paula Fleming

Writing, by its very nature, is a solitary pursuit. It's the writer, the source material and the insistently blinking cursor on the computer screen, waiting for the next keystroke.

But this assignment was different. I became the third partner in Pat and Will's long-term collaboration. And I have to say we made a pretty good team. We came to this project with a common purpose and complementary skills—which is what this book is all about. They had the right contacts; they knew the CHROs and Marketing heads who were trying new ideas, who had found success working together. With my background in training and communications, I had the skills to interview our thought leaders and weave their words into stories.

A comment from contributor Stu Kantor convinced me of my role as storyteller.

He was thinking about the question he wanted to pose for Pat and Will when he said, "I love stories. I learn best from personal stories." His remark made me think that all of us learn best from stories. How many times have you asked, when trying to understand a new concept, "Can you tell me how it works? Can you give me an example?" Case studies—a major teaching technique in law, medical and business schools—are really just stories dressed up in Ivy League suits.

To tell a good story, a writer needs good content. As the writer on this project, I had the benefit of working with a remarkable group of people who had great ideas to share. They were more than generous with their time and candid about their experiences. Their feedback on my drafts invariably improved the final result. And it was gratifying to see how frequently they touched on some of the same themes and reinforced each other's ideas. That convinced me that Pat and Will were on to something with real potential.

Near the end of my writing, I met with Len Vickers to get the final edits on his chapter. As we were wrapping up, Len asked me about the process we were using to put the book together. He thought for a moment and said, "You're really an oral historian. You interview people, record their responses and then write their stories for a larger audience."

His remark took me aback at first. Storyteller was one thing, but oral historian? It sounded a little lofty for what I had been doing. The phrase brought to mind anthropologists capturing moments in time, like the civil rights movement. But the more I thought about it, the more I saw his point. And his comment helped me focus on the final piece of this project, our readers.

"Story matters here" is the tagline cable channel AMC uses to promote its programming. Story matters here, as well. Stories have the power to bring people in, to engage them and, ideally, inspire them. My hope is that these stories will capture the imagination of

readers in our target audience—HR and Marketing professionals—
and inspire them to put their heads together and try some of the
ideas from our team of experts.

And I hope that, before long, they have their own stories to tell.

Inspiration and Practical Advice from the Real World

"The new 'power couple' inside the best companies is an ironclad partnership between marketing leadership and HR leadership. Your brand is your culture, your culture is your brand."

That observation comes from Bill Taylor, co-founder of "Fast Company" and writer of *Harvard Business Review's* popular management blog. It's also the premise of this book.

Working together for a number of years, co-authors Pat Nazemetz and Will Ruch experienced firsthand the power of that partnership. As VP of Human Resources for Xerox, Pat brought in Will, head of the branding and marketing firm Versant, to work together on employee engagement. Their complementary skills and perspectives proved to be a winning combination.

When Pat retired from Xerox in 2011, she and Will opted to continue their partnership. Together they identified more than two dozen practitioners who shared their convictions about the power of HR and Marketing collaborating. These contributors tell their stories in an easy and engaging conversational style. But there is much to learn.

HR professionals may be surprised to discover how much influence they actually exert over their company's brand. How the strength of the brand affects talent recruiting and retention. And why taking a more external view of their work can increase their strategic relevance.

For Marketing professionals, there's an opportunity to see how important the internal brand is, and why it matters to the external brand. There's advice on effective ways to transform employees into ambassadors for your brand.

The partnership of HR and Marketing is good for the workplace and good for the marketplace.

About the Partnership

Patricia M. Nazemetz is Principal of NAZ DEC, a talent consultancy specializing in executive succession strategies. She was formerly Chief Human Resource and Ethics Officer for Xerox Corporation. In her 32-year Xerox career, Pat earned a national reputation for her breakthrough thinking on compensation and benefits, the elements of total pay. But her real passion is talent—how to attract, retain and develop the talent required to drive the organization's success. Pat serves on the boards of WMS Industries, Inc., an electronic gaming and amusement company, and Catholic Health Services of Long Island, a network of not-for-profit hospitals. She is also a member of the Board of Trustees of Fordham University, her alma mater, and of the Corporate Advisory Board of the Carey Business School at Johns Hopkins University.

Will Ruch is CEO and Managing Partner of Versant, Inc., a marketing communications firm that is the winner of several "Best Places to Work" awards as well as the National Psychologically Healthy Workplace Award from the American Psychological Association. Will brings a client-centric approach to all aspects of Versant's business, whether it's building the strategy for high-impact marketing campaigns or helping companies leverage their internal communications to align employees and drive results. He is an engaging speaker, having presented at more than 100 national conferences, including the Association for Corporate Growth (ACG), the National Retail Federation and the Society for Human Resource Management. He serves on various boards, including ACG.

Pat and Will's partnership began during Pat's tenure as head of Xerox's Human Resources for CEO Anne Mulcahy. For the better part of a decade, they worked together on a number of successful employee engagement and communications initiatives. Pat and Will continued their partnership after her retirement from Xerox in 2011. Their experience in bringing together HR knowledge and Marketing creativity provided the inspiration for this book.

Visit our Web site to explore the ideas and services that can help you translate the *HR and Marketing Power Partners* learning into results for you and your organization.

CONSULTING:

Providing strategic thinking and practical guidance to leaders and their organizations, the authors translate the promise of the Power Partnership into engagement, retention, organizational growth and positive brand profile.

PRODUCTS:

Our products help leaders and their teams transform the authors' innovative thinking and experience into "Right People. Right Message." talent and brand results.

- Workshops & Learning
- Customized Career Web Sites, Digital Platforms & Social Media
- "Right Fit" Talent
- Quick Pulse Surveys

SPEAKING:

Through dynamic, interactive, multimedia presentations, the authors bring to life their insights on the HR and Marketing partnership. Their collective experience as speakers has reached thousands of groups and individuals, providing audience members with an inspiring experience that translates into practical action.

For more information, go to:

www.hrmarketingpartners.com